AF431634

From St. John to St. James

and to the End of the World

by Jorg Kristijan Petrovic

Copyright © 2024 by Jorg Kristijan Petrovic

All rights reserved. No part of this publication may be reproduced, distributed, or transmitted in any form or by any means, including photocopying, recording, or other electronic or mechanical methods, without the prior written permission of the author, except in the case of brief quotations embodied in critical reviews and certain other noncomercial uses permitted by copyright law.

ISBN: 979-8-9911265-8-8 (Paperback)

First edition, AD 2024

I dreamed that one day I will be at the same place as the girl on this photo. She was of course long gone when my Camino brought me there. I do not know who she is. I do not even know who is the author of the photography. But I do know that this was my motivational photography through all of my trainings for the 800+ kilometres walk - the walk that I made in the Spring of 2019.

At the crossroads look for the ancient paths and walk in it,
and you will find rest for your souls.

Jeremiah 6.16

To my Trinity: Pia Veronika, Josipina Julija and Izabela Justina

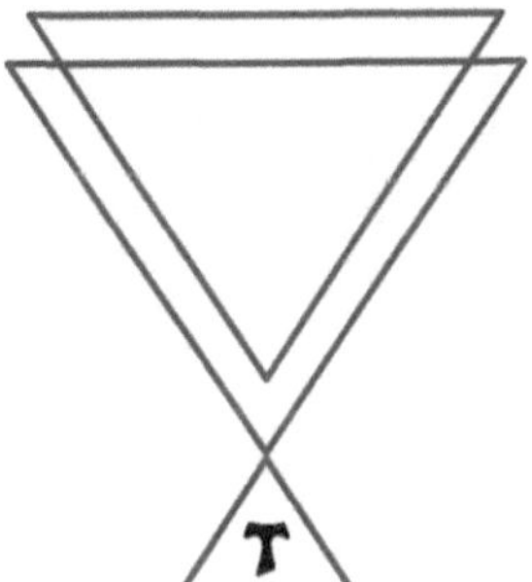

Foreword

By Dr Laima Liucija Andrikienė

'*The Way*'. How many meanings this word has! It has a much deeper meaning than the simple one of an engineering structure or a route for driving, travelling, or walking.

The book you are holding in your hands is about the *Way*, about walking the *Way*. This book, which I have been looking forward to, is about the real meaning of the pilgrimage route, the Saint James Way, Camino de Santiago, and pilgrimage in general, an old tradition from the early Middle Ages. It answers the question why we, the community of media, artificial intelligence, avatars, bubbles, the post-truth society, still need the *Way*, *Camino*, and whether we really need it.

…The St. James Way, often referred to as the Camino, is also known as Europe's oldest and longest street. A street which, more than many other phenomena, expresses the spirit of Europe and our communion, Europe's Christian roots. The Way is a symbol of Christian Europe. Like the most important symbol of the European Union, its flag, twelve gold stars on a blue background, which stands for much more than unity, solidarity, and harmony, or, as people try to explain, the number of countries, the number of apostles of Jesus or the number of months in the year. The designer of the flag, Arsene Heitz (1908-1989), did indeed say what inspired him to create this flag design, it was an image of the Virgin Mary, and so the European Union flag features the twelve golden stars of Our Lady's crown as depicted in the Book of Revelation.

…The Way has another characteristic: people meet on the Way. The author of the book, my colleague at the European Court of Auditors, Delegated Member of the Court from Slovenia, Jorg Kristijan Petrovič talks about the people he has met on the way and what led them to join the pilgrimage. Some of them go in search of God, in search of holiness, others in search of strength and peace of mind after dramas or tragedies that have befallen them or their loved ones, and still others in the hope of finding an answer what path to follow and the goals to achieve. The Way is full of prayers, hopes, petitions to God, encounters, and break-ups. And attempts to discover our world, to better understand the reality around us.

…I recently read a novel that astonished me with its insights into the future. It is a novella by E. M. Forester, first published in 'The Oxford and Cambridge Review' in 1909. I think it is more shocking today than when it first appeared. In the novella, entitled 'The Machine Stops', the author depicts a world in which people live in underground rooms, communicating almost exclusively through the all-powerful machine. This communication is described as "communication by pneumatic mail', which we call 'e-mail' today, and 'picture telephones', which we call 'teleconferencing' or online meetings today. In that future, everywhere can be reached quickly by aircraft, but there is no longer any need or desire to travel, because all over the world cities, hotels, restaurants, shops etc. are similar. Direct and truly human contact is minimal because people are only concerned with their personal convenience. Direct contact with another human being is too exhausting, the family is no longer necessary, and religion is seen as a relic of an earlier time. People worship the Great Machine that they themselves created. Fear of confronting of some inconvenience drives most people to choose euthanasia rather than face old age. At the end of this literary vision, the Great Machine breaks down, but people are no longer able to communicate or survive without it. After reading such a work, one can seriously think about what kind of 'progress' we have made in the last century. The real challenge is to choose the way that will lead us to the future we want. Also, a future dreamed by the founders of the European Union.

…The third decade of the 21st century is halfway through. The computer, the internet, Facebook, Twitter, LinkedIn have become inseparable attributes of our lives, replacing handwritten letters and postcards, and, increasingly, conversations, not only on the phone, but conversations in general. Monosyllabic new words, short phrases, are becoming sufficient for communication between people. We live in an age of communication. Except that our communication is a kind of one-armed communication: we send a message and do not wait for a reply; there is communication, but no dialogue. We already have robots cleaning our houses, robots mowing our lawns, drones looking after our cows in the pastures; these days, in Phoenix, Arizona (USA), we have driverless cars driving around the streets: the driver's seat is empty, the passengers are sitting in the back seat, and the car is being driven by an invisible robot. In a couple of years, industrialists say, these cars will be on our streets too. Not to mention automated accounting and control systems, robots in factories, ports and elsewhere. We no longer know how to live without iPhones, iPads, WhatsApp, and the rest. Robots live in our homes, our kitchens, our bedrooms, our hospitals, our fields, our seas, our forests, our skies...

Does a modern person, who lives surrounded by such technologies and devices and robots, still need the Way of Saint James? Does he still care about the old traditional pilgrimage? In a world of excess, where excess and poverty somehow successfully coexist side by side, is there still room for things of the spirit, higher matters? Maybe we don't need it anymore? Maybe all we have left is a rush, an eternal hunger for information, knowledge, technology, new and fresh, the creation and protection of a comfort zone? And the rest is ballast, re-living, history, simply - the past, which should remain there?... It turns out - no. It turns out that today's man needs things that nourish and strengthen the spirit even more than before. Maybe that's why we notice that pilgrimage is experiencing a renaissance, that the young - not only the older and the old - need God, they need the Camino de Santiago, the Way of Saint James. The desire to understand and master new technologies is perfectly compatible with the desire to seek God and understand His plan; it is compatible with the desire to know the past, cultural heritage, to understand other peoples with whom we share the world; the desire to get to know the world view, customs and traditions of people who look different and speak different languages, to understand what makes us different and what makes us similar. After all, the world has become so small, there must be enough space for all of us in it, we must learn to live and coexist in that shrunken world.

...*The Way* brings people together and separates them. I am one of the pilgrims of the St James Way, having walked the Way and been to the Cathedral of Santiago de Compostela many times. And always looking for opportunities to return. *The Way* has also allowed me to get to know Jorg Kristijan Petrovič, a professional and experienced auditor, but more importantly, above all, a person who upholds Christian values and traditions, and who, in his personal life, manifests human values and all Europe's good qualities.

Dear Jorg Kristijan, don't get tired along the *Way*. *Buen camino*, dear pilgrim! *Ultreia o ultreya!*

Luxembourg, 20 June 2024

 Laima Liucija Andrikienė is Lithuanian Delegated Member of the European Court of Auditors. Since 2022 she lives and works in Luxembourg.

Economist mathematician by training and graduate of Vilnius University, she has been Member of the European Parliament (2004-2014, 2016-2019), Member of the Seimas (Parliament) of Lithuania (1990-2000, 2020-2022), Minister of European Affairs of Lithuania (1996-1998).

Laima Andrikienė is a Signatory of the Act of the Restoration of Independence of Lithuania (11 March 1990).

She is the author of more than 100 publications in Lithuanian, Russian, English, Polish and French on economics, politics, privatisation, economic reform, security, human rights, and Christian values.

Dr Laima Andrikienė is editor and co-author of the scientific monograph "Contemporary Tendencies of Lobbying" (Vilnius, 2002), author and editor of the book "The Light of St. James Way" (in Lithuanian & English; Vilnius, 2012, 2013, 2014), co-author and co-editor of "Values and Politics II. Christian Roots of Europe" (in Lithuanian & English; Vilnius, 2014). Among other books is "Europe's Sunset is Cancelled" (with Arnas Ališauskas; Vilnius, 2019).

She is widely known and acknowledged for the establishment (2013) of St James Way network in Lithuania which includes four internationally recognised and certified pilgrim routes. The patron of the network is HE Gintaras Grušas, the Archbishop Metropolitan of Vilnius. Since 2016, traditional hiking of young pilgrims, Ambassadors of St

James Way, whose number is approaching 10,000, every year takes place in Lithuania from May to July.

Acros the Pyrenees

Palm Sunday of 2019 was on April 14th. This was the day when I started to walk my Camino in Saint Jean Pied de Port.

I started my walk after a mass in a SJPP church. It was a spring day. Some trees there were already blooming. Up on the Pyrenees, there was still some snow lying around. Especially on the Spanish side as there is no warm breeze from The Bay of Biscay as in SJPP.

My first stop was at the Ferme Ithurburia, a little pub shortly after the big curve. I had my first morning coffee there. There I meet people that I already meet on the road. A couple from Belgium and a family from the USA. Grandfather of the American family was a geologist and as I showed him my stone for the Cruz the Ferro (a volcanic tuff) he told me all about its minerals. He actually knew the place where I picked the stone. He was in the Kamniška bistrica valley near Kamnik in Slovenia years ago and knew all about its geology.

Just before Refuge Orisson I met Pascal from Germany and just a little bit later Rhian and Layke from Denmark. At the big tree some pilgrims left a little cross just to remind us about our Lord Jesus Christ.

Pascal from Germany became one of my best friends on the Camino. He was the first one of my German speaking groups that I met on the Camino. A group I walked with in my first week on the Camino. I walked with Pascal for the next couple kilometres. He made the first movie of me walking the Camino. After about an hour we split since I decided to climb my first Pyrenees peak. Besides, I was a much slower walker than Pascal. It was early afternoon, and the weather was still fine. So, I took myself time to enjoy the mountains. People of Slovenia are a mountain nation since part of our country lies in the Alps. So, mountains are no problem for us. I was physically well prepared, and my plan was from the beginning not just to walk the 26km etapa to Roncesvalles but also to climb to all the Pyrenees peaks along the Camino. The Sceneries were fantastic. Next time I met Pascal was a day later. We happen to be in the same hostel in Zubiry.

After coming down from the first Pyrenees peak and a prayer at Maria I continued my walk toward the Cruz de Thibault. There are lots of horses that graze in mountain pastures in this part of the way.

Cruz de Thibault is not far away from the top of the Pyrenees passage. Just a couple of hundred meters and you are there. As you come to the passage you see a big rock on your left and a small shelter on your right. Weather changes quickly in the Pyrenees and such a shelter can be a lifesaving facility. It is nicely marked with a St James Shell. From this passage on it goes more or less only downwards toward Roncesvalles. But as I came to the passage, I was not about to go down but up.

I had one more peak to climb. The highest one along the way. This is actually a mountain with two peaks. The smaller peak has a pile of rocks on the top and is about 50 meters lower than the top one. It was 5 pm as I came to the top peak, and it started to rain. Since it was a Palm Sunday, I was carrying with me the traditional Slovenian Palm Sunday green called "Butarica" – a bundle of spring greens.

I have left it on the top of the mountain as a reminder that one Slovenian pilgrim was here. Then I quickly left the top since in the rain, even if it is only early spring or late winter up here, you never know about the lightning.

Along the way, just under the highest peak, every pilgrim passes a big stone slab with the first distance information. It says 765 km to Santiago de Compostela. Long way to go. And a little bit further down the road another sign at the Roland fountain that reminds you that you are already in Spain in Navara. From there on I entered an enchanted forest. It was really mystical. Very calm. No bird songs. No wind. Totally silent. Full of fog and still partly covered with snow. The path there goes along the ridge. Some time on its left side, some time on its right side. I was alone. No pilgrims were here anymore. It was already late afternoon, and everybody was already in Roncesvalles. I saw another shelter. This one was a modern one. It also had a fireplace so you can warm yourself up if caught in a snowstorm.

Just a little bit before you got the first glimpse of the Roncesvalles there is an emergency telephone. Another help for pilgrims caught in storms. In my case it was also a point where clouds started to disappear, and sun came out again. From here on you descend via an old curvy road. Sceneries are fantastic. Roncesvalles looks just like you can just reach it with your hand. But it is still some way to go.

In an hour I was down in the valley and at that moment it started to get dark. Luckily, I had a headlight.

As I came to Roncesvalles monastery it was 9.45 pm and it was already dark night. As I asked for a bed they told me I was lucky that they had only one left. Only later I found out that earlier during the day they sent many pilgrims further on to the next village since they had the information from SJPP how many were on the way. In every hostel they have a policy to leave some beds for late comers since they are usually the ones that are the most exhausted and need the bed most. It was the Holy week and many people were on the Way of Saint James. Especially many pilgrims from Spain since as I understand Holy Week Is a public holiday in Spain.

Roncesvalles monastery hostel is one of the best on the whole way. I believe it is also the biggest one. It was renovated just recently, and it looks great.

I got the bed, but the kitchen was unfortunately already closed. So, no supper. Luckily, I still had some bread and cheese. I made a sandwich, and it tasted great. As I ate it up it was already 10 pm and the lights went off. I went to the bathroom where I met Herman that I knew already from the train to SJPP. He told me that Sandra was already asleep, and he introduced me to two of his Spanish friends – Juanlu and Antonio.

I did the laundry and took it downstairs to put it on the rack to dry. Something that I will do many times in the next four weeks.

So my first day on the Camino came to its end. I was happy everything was OK. No blisters, no muscle pain. All the peaks conquered. Roncesvalles rached. Bed I got.

It was a perfect day and I slept like an angel.

I got a bed and a candy

Second day started early. It was still dark as I went to the building where they serve hostel breakfast - La Posada. We were 5 at the table. An American couple, a lady from Canada, Richard, and me. Richard was from Spain but since I do not speak Spanish we talked in English. He was about to do the whole Camino just like me. He's plan was to make it in 4 weeks. My plan was to make it in 4 and a half weeks. He was younger than me and very athletic so I had no doubt he will succeed. I met him many more times later on the Camino. I was most happy that we also met at the end in Santiago de Compostela for dinner. But that morning at my first Camino breakfast I didn't know all that jet. But I knew one thing, that I just got a friend, a very good friend!

There were many more things that I didn't knew that day. For example, that a little girl and her father that are sitting at the next breakfast table are going to be in my German speaking group in five days from now (Father's name was Sasha and little girl's name was Lea). And I did not know that two girls that I saw at Burguete and later on some little stone slab bridge were Lucia and Coral who will later be a part of the same group as my new friend Richard. I also didn't know that the three girls near the pillar water crossing are going to be the second three girls that I will meet that afternoon in Zubiri and that one of them will take a good picture of me with the famous Zubiri bridge. I also didn't know that this afternoon there will be no beds in Zubiri.

So, after breakfast I started the walk of my second day on the Camino. It was a nice day, and I was full of energy. But before you start to walk you have to take the first traditional photo of the Camino. A photo with the road sign that says 790 km to Santiago de Compostela.

After the "must do" picture I made a phone call to my daughter Josipina Julija. Today was her 16th birthday. Then I started to walk.

As I came to Zubiri at 5.40 pm I saw 3 girls that I had met on the Camino already in the morning. They were slacking at the famous bridge, and it seems they don't know what to do. I asked one of them if she could take a picture of me with the famous bridge. »Shure no problem«. Picture was not good since I was cowering practically the whole bridge with my body.

So, I decided to cross the famous bridge even though the Camino follows the river on this side. The Middle Ages legend about rabies must have been an excellent business. Back then you had to pay to go across the bridge. And the fees for bridges with the legends must have cost extra. Today of course you can cross the bridge for free.

On the other side of the bridge other 3 girls are lying in the grass, stretching their muscles.

I asked one of them to photograph me with the bridge and she did a great job. Sometimes the worlds on two sides of the river are light years away. Or it might just be that the light on the other side was better. But enough about the light. In the meantime, as I was chasing the good motive of myself with the Zubiri bridge, the sky went dark grey. It looks like the storm is coming up the valley. My final destination today is another 5 kms down the road. Should I go and get wet with rain or should I simply stay in Zubir and not reach my today's goal. I decided to stay.

I pull out the list of telephone numbers of the hostels on the Camino. The list is given to every pilgrim in SJPP along with the credentials. I call the first hostel. No vacancy. I call in the second. No spare beds there. Third. Sorry all full. It all looks like I will have to go on. I call to Larrasoana. Nothing there either. And to the next village. Same, they have no beds left. And Pamplona is 20 kilometres away. No go, even if there was no rain coming. What now? No plan B. Shit!

Many pilgrims are on the Camino today. It is the first day after Palm Sunday. The holy week attracts many people from Spain to come on the Camino. But not just them. On the Camino it is just like in summer. In the afternoon everybody is already in the hostels. If you don't come early - no bed 4 you.

As I am thinking about these facts a beard man comes over the bridge. I ask him if he is looking for a bed as well. He says that he is just coming back from Larrasoana, since there were no beds and the locals advised him to go 5 km back to Zubiri since it is a larger village. I tell him that I have already called all the hostels and that there are no vacant beds here. I joke that, since it looks like rain is coming, we might have to sleep under the famous bridge. By sleeping the whole night there we will not get resistant just to rabies but to all the other diseases too. He is not in a joking mood, so he does not smile. No »always look on the bride side of life…« there. O, go to hell. So you walked five kilometres to Larrasoana and five back. And now you are in a bad mood. Why didn't you use a phone? Really smart. So smart it makes me angry. I better leave. So I tell him I am going to the nearest shop to buy some supplies. He goes there as well.

I buy two litters of orange juice and start to pack them in front of the shop. He comes out of the shop with an idea: Why don't we go to the police station to ask if we could sleep in the prison. I explain him that the idea to punch him and start a fight crossed my mind a while ago. If I did, we would have definitely got our accommodation problem solved by the police. He does not like this joke either. First rain drops start to fall from the sky. They are big and very wet. So, we both run around the corner in the direction of the police station. Maybe the idea might work. Luck is on the side of the brave or in our case maybe it is better to say luck is on the side of the fools. As we come around the corner the rain is already very strong. And I can't believe my eyes, there is a hostel right there around the corner. The very one that my companion has heard about in Larrasoana an hour ago. The one that might still have some beds left. I called them fifteen minutes ago and they were full of guests - but who knows. Hope dies last. The receptionist tells us right away that they do not have any vacant beds. So we sit down on the bench in the garage and wait for the rain shower to go by.

Five minutes later the receptionist tells us that there might actually be four beds left. Two girls in the dining room are already waiting for two of those beds. That we might get the other two beds if we wait for another hour. The beds have been reserved by four Italians and if they do not show up by 7.30pm she will give the beds to us. In case the Italians do show up, she will take the two girls with her car to Pamplona where she lives. The two of us on the other hand will have to order a cab to Pamplona since all the buses have already left. We are sure that we are having the beds since no one comes to the hostel this late. We go to the dining room to wait. The receptionist gives each of us a bottle of beer and we toast. It looks like we are really the lucky ones to get the beds in this situation where there are no beds left in the whole valley between Roncesvalles and Pamplona.

Ten minutes later Italians are at the front door, and we are on the street again.

I empty my beer and say to the beard men that it does not rain under the bridge. Another bad joke. He looks at me like he is already having rabies. He would probably like to throw me down from that damn bridge. But that would mean that he would get a free bed for the next 30 years. So he doesn't say or do anything and our accommodation problem remains unsolved.

We are getting ready to get out of the hostel. The prison idea is now out of the question since the receptionist managed to persuade us that it is totally crazy.

As we step outside it rains like cats and dogs. I go to the right to see if there is any bench at the bus station. The beard man goes back to the shop since he has forgotten his walking poles there.

There is no bench at the bus station. But it has a roof two by four meter large so at least the rain is not pouring on you.

As I think about the possible solutions, the beard man comes around the corner. I do not know if he has found his walking poles, but I see he has found two ladies.

Jeane and Christine are looking for a bed too. So now we are four. It is clear to me - we have no chance.

And right at this moment the first 3 bridge-photo girls appear from somewhere.

I tell them I am looking for a bed. »Sure no problem.« again. They explain that they are just returning from some hostel, where they have had a great supper with their friends and that in that hostel there is a vacant bed. One (1) bed! The beard men and two ladies are delighted about the news.

So, all four of us went toward that hostel. It's raining. It is getting dark. It is cold. It is wet. We are four. And the bed is only for one person.

Fifty meters later I turn into the pub at the local sports center. They continue to walk in the rain toward the hostel. I have to think about the situation. If all four of us show up at the hostel, no one will get the bed. If three of them show up at the hostel, the hostel receptionist is still going to be in a tough moral dilemma. It is always "Ladies first!", so the man with the beard has no chance. But choosing between two ladies, who on top happen to be good friends, is impossible too. You can not give the bed only to one of them. So in my opinion the three of them have no chance. The bed is for one person only and none of them is going to get it.

In the pub of the local sports hall, I ordered a tea and let my phone charge. TV on the wall shows footage from Paris where Notre Dame cathedral is swallowed in flames. Shortly before 10pm the bartender comes to charge for the tea. They are closing. I will have to leave.

I exit the pub and put on my rain jacket. I go through my options. Shall I go sleep under the famous bridge after all? With such heavy rain, who knows how high the river might rise? It might be risky to sleep there. I know I saw some dry entrances to an old hostel that is currently under renovation, so I could sleep there on the floor. At least I will be in a dry place. But first I decided to try my luck at the hostel with a single bed.

Hostel is not far away. Maybe a five minutes' walk. Nord by the main road and then left into a small street. It is the third house on the right side of the little street. I enter the garden and knock on the door. Nobody answers. So I knock on the window of the kitchen. A young lady opens the window and I ask if they have any beds left. She tells me that all the beds are taken. I am desperate and she is desperate to. She asks me to wait a second and comes to open the door. She lets me in the garage. Walking shoes are on the shelves and raincoats are on the racks, drying. Walking poles are piled in one corner and a washing machine is doing the laundry in the other corner. And there is a bench where you can sit down when you are putting your shoes on or off.

She sits me there on the bench and asks if I would like a bowl of hot soup. I am grateful for such an offer since a hot soup is going to warm me. It got actually pretty chilly outside.

As she brings me the soup, she explains to me that the whole valley is in some kind of emergency since all the hostels, all the way to Pamplona, are full. This holy week has taken all of them by surprise. Especially because the biggest bed capacity - community hostel in Zubiri - is closed due to renovation. She explains that just half an hour ago they had put three pilgrims in a cab and sent them to Pamplona. Two ladies and a man with a beard.

The soup is great. It is a simple vegetable soup, but it feels like heaven. It is not just the soup; it is the warm approach of the hospitalieros. They are taking care of a lonely pilgrim in the stormy night, and they are doing it really cordially.

As I eat the soup, I am thinking that I should ask them if they would let me sleep here on the bench in the garage.

Five minutes later one of the hospitalieros comes to me and invites me to the dining room where all the other pilgrims have dinner. She explains that I should have dinner and, in the meantime, they will find me a place to sleep.

In the dining room there are two large tables. Some eight to ten people are sitting at each of them. The first person I recognize is Pascal, so I sit down right next to him. He introduced me to all the other guests. At our table I meet Rosvita and Monika, from Germany; Damian and Andrew, father and son; Bayron and Janete from Canada and Tess from Ireland.

Tess is sitting next to me on my left and Pascal is sitting on my right. By the next table sits Helmut from Germany and talks to Jozhi, Waldy (Ewaldine) and Maya, three ladies in their sixties, all of them coming from the Netherlands. There were also other pilgrims at the table, but I am sorry I do not remember all the names. Experience was pretty intense so I do remember some names and lots of details of that evening as you dear reader can see, but unfortunately not all of them.

Dinner is perfect. We eat meat and potatoes and there is a bottle of wine on the table. Everybody gets a glass of wine. Later on I learned that this is a custom in Spain. Even if you order just a glass of wine you will get the whole bottle and no matter how much of that bottle you drink you will pay 1 or 2 euros for that bottle which is a great price - at least according to my wine prices experiences back at home in Slovenia.

After the main dish we all get a great desert. One can choose between fruits and yogurt with honey. I go for honey. I am exhausted and I need some sugar for energy. I do not know what to expect. It might be a tough night. Hopefully at least on the bench in the garage. But it might also be in that dry entrance of the closed hostel. I comfort myself that I have at least got an excellent warm supper and that my sleeping bag is filled with down so that I will not suffer from too much cold.

It is already past 11pm. So I modestly ask the hospitalieros if she has managed to find me some place where I am going to spend the night. She smiles and points to a couch. »Mr. Jorg, you are going to sleep on that couch. You are sharing this dining room with Rosvita and Monika, who have got that other two couches there at the window.« I am shocked – in a positive way of course. But that is not the end of the story. Things got even better.

Tess, who is sitting next to me, tells me: »Jorg, you are to big for this couch! If you help me bring down my stuff from the room you can get my bed. I will sleep on the couch.« »Besides« she laughs »You cannot share the room with two ladies.«. I cannot believe my ears. I thank her with all my heart.

In less than a minute we go up to pick up her stuff. In the dormitory there are two bunks. On the bunk at the window two pilgrims are already sleeping. The bed that Tess is giving me is the lower one of the bunk standing right next to the door.

Tess passes me her backpack and starts to pack a suitcase. I am puzzled about the amount of the luggage, so I asked her how she carries all this stuff. Does she put the backpack on her shoulders and carry the suitcase in her hand? That looks pretty heavy to me. Only then did I learn from her explanation that there are some kind of post services that delivers your luggage from one hostel to the other for something like 3 or 4 euros.

I bring down Tess's backpack. As she comes down too, I thank her again. She explains that she knows that I am a real pilgrim. On the other hand, she is planning not just to use the post-delivery for the luggage but also means of transportation. Her vacation is short so she must be in Compostela in two weeks. So, she felt I need that bed more than she does. She also explains that she has decided to do at least one good deed every day.

As we sipped the final glass of wine Tess insists, I should make reservations for the next couple of days. I follow her advice and make hostel reservations for the next three days. First one in Pamplona, the second one in Puente la Reina and the third one in Estella.

In the meantime, Pascal is talking to Helmut and they ask me if I am going to join them tomorrow on the walk toward Pamplona. We agree to start at 5.30. So, it is time to go to sleep and we all go to our rooms.

As I come to my bed I found in the middle of it a candy waiting for me. I show it to Helmut who is in the upper bed of the bunk. We can not believe our eyes. Tess is really an angel.

And Camino is about people like Tess. People of modesty, of willingness to help and of people with lots of good will.

And the candy? It went with me all the way to the end of the
world – to Finistere where the very last milestone with the
famous Km 0,000 mark stands.

In Pamplona my German speaking group formed

Third day started early. Just as planned Pascal, Helmut and I started to walk at 6 and we stopped for the first coffee at 9.40 at La Prada de Zuriain. It was there where I took a picture of the second 3 girls from Zubiri. From here it is only 11 km to Pamplona. Helmut and Pascal continued in their fast rhythm, but I shifted to a lower gear. I am not able to walk at a German pace. I am a slow walker.

Still, it was only midday when I came to Burlada which is a suburb of Pamplona. First, I took a picture with the famous bridge over river Ulzama at Basilica de la Santisima Trinidad de Arre and then I entered the main street of Burlada. And as I came to the first plaza, I heard a group of people greeting me. It was Richard and his friends: Lucia, Coral, Albert, Jordi, Aleix, Maria. It was great to meet Richard again. I met him for the second time in my life, but it felt like we knew each other since forever. He introduced me to his friends, and we spoke for a while. Then I had to go on. First stop Pharmacy. It is interesting that I got no blisters on my first day despite all the climbing on the Pyrenees peaks, but on my second day which was basically only a descent from Roncesvalles to Zubiri I earned two blisters. And today they started to grow. I had my Compeed patches, but I knew I will need a lot more in the coming days and I needed an adhesive tape to fix the patches since their own adhesive is not strong enough – at least not after 6 hours of continuous walk – and they tend to migrate away from the blister. Pharmacy was not far from where I met Richard and his friends. It is funny when you enter the pharmacy, Compeed is all over the place, on the left on the right in front and at the back. They really know what you will come for.

With a new stock of blister fighting equipment, I continued to the nearby Pamplona. First, I went to the cathedral where the Navara kings and queens are buried and then to a different kind of king – to the Burger King. I was hungry and I was hungry for meat. I took the biggest whopper and large French fries - and they came with a gift. Sunglasses with a red frame.

These sunglasses looked silly but on the other hand they might also have come from some modern fancy designer. So, on second thought I decided I will wear them and as I exited the BK I put them on. From there I went toward the main plaza since the hostel where I made my reservation was on the other side of the town. But I didn't come far.

On the main plaza – Plaza Del Castillo - someone called my name again. This time it were Helmut and Pascal. They were sitting at Café Iruña having a beer. I joined them of course and ordered one for myself. After so many kilometers I have earned one. After all, it was also a great dessert on top of the hamburger.

Helmut and Pascal introduced me to Martin from Switzerland who was with them at the table and was in the same hostel as they were. We sat there for hours and talked. I only left for half an hour just to put my backpack in the hostel. Helmut gave me a tour in the Café Iruña and told me all about it. Café Iruña has been a famous place in Pamplona for decades. Ernest Hemingway (a Nobel prize awarded writer from the USA - he was awarded with it for "The old men and the sea", thou in my opinion he has deserved it for the "Farewell to arms") sat here at the bar in his yearly visits to Pamplona almost 100 years ago. He definitely got the ideas for his book "The Sun Also Rises" here.

That afternoon Helmut told us that this is his second Camino. Later as we became a group, I always saw him as a kind of group leader since he was the most experienced. On many occasions he has shown that his experiences are highly valued. Without them we would not get our beds, or we would treat blisters completely wrong. He was a great man and a true friend. So was Martin and of course Pascal whom I knew from my first hours on the Camino. I knew that they are all good people and that they would be my good friends in the next couple of days on the Camino, but then in Pamplona I could never imagine that we would be friends all the way to the end of the world. But how should I, at that time Finistere was 29 days and more than 700 km away.

So, we were there on the Plaza Del Castillo in front of Café Iruña drinking beer. Four men. Two from Germany. One from Switzerland. And one from Slovenia. It was spring. It was sunny. It was a perfect afternoon.

On Wednesday the 17th of April 2019 I left Pamplona - a city that runs with the bulls.

That morning I slept as long as it was allowed in the Aloha hostel. Their policy was luckily not so strict as in community hostels. I needed to sleep since after 3 days of walking I felt a little bit fatigued. I caught the last half an hour of breakfast. Aleks from Australia that slept on the upper part of the bunk was already gone. We only talked briefly last night before we all went to sleep. Alex was a very quiet and closed-in person. She had a lot of self-made tattoos on her hands. They spoke for the life she had. It must have been a pretty tough life. But she was here on the Camino taking care of it. Still, it looks like that life she had has taught her not to say too much. Days later I met her in Logronio. As we met, I called her by her name. »Oh, you have remembered my name!« she said and smiled. I was glad to see her smiling.

It was a smile of honest happiness. It means a lot to the people if you care to remember their names. That is why I tried really hard to remember the names of the people I met on the Camino. Unfortunately, I do not remember them all.

The story of my staff

At breakfast I met Andrej. He was the first of the two people from Slovenia that I met on the whole Camino. We are a small nation of only 2 million and on an average year it is not more than 700 Slovenian citizens that do the Camino. And I guess most of them are there in summer. So, it is not unusual that I met only two.

Today's etapa was up to Alto de Perdon and then down to Puente la Reina. Alto de Perdon is special because of its pilgrim's monument – in iron cut figures of the pilgrims through the centuries. Definitely one of the best pictures sites along the Camino. I went out of Pamplona alone but already halfway to Alto de Perdon I met German, Sandra, Marta, Antonio and Juanlu. German and Sandra were my first friends on the Camino. We met actually before we started to walk the Camino, as we sat together on the same Saturday evening train to Saint Jean Pied de Port, 5 days ago. German introduced me to his friends Antonio and Juanlu back in Roncesvalles. But Marta I met anew.

German, Sandra, Marta, Antonio and Juanlu were a lovely group and I was really happy to see them again. They have teased me about my pilgrim's stick since it was really big and clumsy. But I liked my stick since it was a gift from my friends.

A little bit further up the road, in the village called Zariquiegui, I met my friend Richard again. It was a loud "Hello Richard my friend!" and the same loud "Hello Jorg!" back, an obligatory "Buen Camino!" followed by "How are you today?" and of course a strong friendly hug. It was after all a reunion of the old friends – friends that have known each other for 3 long days already. It is funny, but time has a different dimension on Camino. Richard was not alone. His group was already departing up to the hill so we parted. But only for half an hour.

I came up to the Alto de Perdon as Richard's group was there already taking pictures. I asked them if they could help me with my pictures and they did. They also started to ask me about my pilgrim staff so I decided to tell them its story.

The staff is a gift from my friends from middle school. As I turned 50 in January this year (2019) they gave it to me as a birthday present. They really made an effort. They went to our local valleye of Kamniška bistrica to get a special wood. It is called Gold rain.

One of my friends studied forestry and he knows all about trees and woods. Gold rain (Laburnum alpinum) is poisonous so you can't make spoons or anything like this out of it, but it is ideal for hard tasks since it is the hardest European wood. Peoples of Europe used Laburnum wood for centuries before hard African wood came and became more fashionable. In Scotland for example pipes – the famous music instrument of the Highlands - were made of Gold rain wood. It is a great wood not just because it is so hard but especially because it is resistant to rottening and no insects can do it any harm. So already the very wood of my staff is special.

The trunks and the branches of Gold rain consist of two parts. They have an inner core that is dark brown and is hard as hell. This inner part is the one that is to be used. But the wood also has the outer part that is white and is not so hard. So, my friend brought the pole wood home and had to cut that outer soft white part away. By doing that Miha almost lost his finger. He cut himself deep and he had to go to the emergency hospital. There was a lot of bleeding and he got quite some stitches, so the project was put on hold for a couple of weeks.

As you can see already in the time of fabrication a lot of suffering happened. So, when I got it I knew, I have to take my part of the suffering. And I did take the staff all the way to Santiago de Compostela and to the end of the world – Finistere. The staff was heavy, clumsy and before everything it was very, very big. But I am big too, and very, very stubborn. I didn't want to quit on my staff, no matter what happened. Not even when I carried it on the back of my backpack, and it started to rain and I could not pull the protection cover over my backpack and the water started to pour inside of my backpack and my robes and my sleeping back got soaking wet. I didn't give up on my staff. It newer even crossed my mind because it brought me so much joy.

The staff namely carried a kind of blessing. It is the story that everybody wanted to hear. I already told you the first part of the story of how my friends got the wood and prepared it. Already the first part about the suffering touches the hearts but the second part is even much deeper because it is about the very soul of the staff.

Together with the staff my friends also gave me a paper that was written with a couple of letters, words and numbers. Some of them are also engraved on the staff's front side that looks like cobra's neck and at its top back side which looks like cobra's head. As I deciphered the engravings on the staff and the numbers written on the paper the stories are as follows.

The first story is about Moses. Moses talked to God and he was afraid that the people of Israel would not believe that he had talked to Him.

So the LORD asked him, "?What is that in your hand?"" A staff," he replied. "Throw it on the ground," said the Lord. So, Moses threw it on the ground, and it became a snake, and he ran from it. "Stretch out your hand and grab it by the tail." the LORD said to Moses. So, he reached out his hand and caught the snake, and it turned back into a staff in his hand. (Exodus 4:2-4)

The second story is carried by the front engravings. There are three letters engraved there: +C+M+B+

The letters stand for Caspar, Melkhiard and Balthazar. The three wise men – the three kings. My friends say that these three were actually pilgrims that have followed the star to the newborn Jesus. And they say that I am also following the star or stars because one of the legends goes that the name of Compostela is from Latin Campo Stelaris – the Field of Stars. Speaking of Latin words, one thing that I know for sure about the Camino is that the whole experience was definitely »Per aspera ad astra«. A lot of physical pain and suffering on the road but at the end you feel celestial.

But back to the stories of my staff. The second meaning of the three (CMB) letters is the one that we chalk above our entry doors on the 6th of January. »!Christy Manesonem Benedicty!« Christ bless this house. And according to the interpretation of my friends the pilgrims also bring the blessing to every house they enter, because they are on a holy mission – on pilgrimage. So, I was supposed to bring blessings on my way. A noble mission but also a mission that can get in your head like a strong wine. And then all of the sudden you start to think that you are something special. Something more. And you totally forget to be humble. My friends are very wise, and they know about these things. That is why they gave me a warning on the back side of the staff.

And this warning is the third story of my staff. On its the back side– the side that has faced my eyes all the time – are engraved the following two letters: MM. They stand for »!Memento Mori!«, meaning remember the death, remember that you are mortal, remember that you are nothing special.

The saying comes from Roman times. When the Roman generals won the battles, they were honoured with the laurel wreath. They were the central point of the parades. The golden carriage drove them through the streets of Rome. The look on them must have been magnificent because it was not just the carriage that shined in gold it was also their uniform. The wreath above their heads also shined in gold.

The wreath was held above their heads by the person that stood behind them on the carriage. But holding the wreath was not the only function of that person. Maybe even more important than holding the wreath, above the head of the victorious Roman general, was the words that this person whispered in the general's ears. During the whole parade through the streets of Rome this person whispered to the general: »Memento Mori.« You are just a mortal, like everybody else, you are not a god from the Roman pantheon.

The intention was to keep the mind of successful people down to *earth* since it was very clear, even 2000 years ago, how quickly things go into person's head. Egos feeds on success and you lose contact with the ground under your feet quicker than you can imagine. I call this the altitude sickness.

So this was the story of my staff that I gave to Richard and his friends. My speech was so intense that at the end they were all silent looking at me. Some of them with mouth open;

not knowing what to say. And only after some moments Lucia, the girl with the pearl earrings, managed to say in a shaking voice full of respect: "Is it allowed to touch this staff?"

This came as a complete surprise for me and I said: "Yes of course it would be an honour to me if I could take a photo of you all holding it." And this is exactly what we did. They all stood in a half circle, holding a staff with one hand and I took the photo. Afterwards they also wanted not just the photo with my staff but with me as well. Taking photos brought us all a lot of fun and everybody relaxed, and it sealed our friendship for all the days that came afterwards. Unfortunately, some of them had to leave the Camino as the holy week came to an end but we still follow each other on social media. They were all great young people, and I am really happy I had the opportunity to meet them. And their reaction to the story of my staff told me that there is something about it. I was sure it was the right decision to bring it with me. Despite the fact that it was not easy to carry, it has brought me a lot of joy, and not just to myself but also to the others.

Pretty soon it became my trademark. People have started to stop me and asked to hear the story. It looks like the story about the pilgrim, who carries a big staff with a story, started to spread around. And stories are important. Good stories are one of the reasons people come to Camino. I become known as the pilgrim with the big staff. Helmut joked I should be called Gandalf from the Lord of the Rings – the "You shall not pass!" one. One of my friends even suggested, that because of its shape, the staff could also be seen as the "Nimbus 2000" from Harry Potter. Anyhow, it started to live its own life on the Camino. It became an object that almost nobody ignored. If I was not approached directly and asked about it, then it was the people talking or just whispering about it. I actually constantly heard: "… staff …", "… stick …", "… pole …", " … baston …", …

This staff is really unique. Miha knew where to cut the wood and almost lost his finger making it. My friends gave it to me as a present. It came with a full list of letters and numbers – mysterious ciphers. It brought me a lot of blessing on the Camino as I was carrying it to the end of the world.

On my way home it was temporarily lost in flight from Santiago de Compostela over Barcelona to Venice. It was delivered to my home in Mercedes Benz days later. I asked the delivery man if they always deliver pilgrim sticks in such noble cars, but he said that only if they expect Gandalf to be the staff's owner. This was of course a joke, he explained later that he is not just delivering lost luggage but that he is also driving passengers to the airport. Nevertheless, the less the fact remains – my pilgrim stick came home in Mercedes Benz.

After we took photos Richard and his friends left for Puente la Reina. At that very moment German, Sandra, Marta, Juanlu and Antonio came to the top of the Alto de Perdon and since I was in photo mode I asked them as well if we could take a photo together. We did that and then I sat down and had a snack. In the meantime, my Spanish friends left and as I was just about to leave too, Tess showed up. Tess that helped me in Zubiri. I was so happy I see her and I thanked her again for all of her kindness. We made another set of pictures and then left Alto de Perdon together. We descended down to Uterga and stopped in Muruzabal for a meal. There at the Table I met Robert from Spain.

After the meal I said goodbye to Robert and Tess. Unfortunately, this was my final goodbye with Tess. I have not met her again. As I came to Puente la Reina it was already late afternoon. I met none of my friends on the main street, so I went straight to my hostel. The hostel where I made a reservation for bed was on the other side of the bridge up on the hill outside of Puente la Reina. A modern big facility. Very clean but with a total lack of soul. Next time I will definitely look for a hostel somewhere down in the town.

I put my backpack down next to my bed and took out some bread, cheese and beer that I just bought down at a little shop on the Puente la Reina main street. With all that stock I went back across the bridge to sit at the riverbank and enjoy the view of the famous bridge. And there I met German, Sandra, Marta, Juanlu and Antonio again. Just as I shared my food and beer with them, my German speaking friends came to the riverbank too. It was Pascal, Helmut and Martin. Three friends that I spent my yesterday's afternoon at Cafe Iruna in Pamplona with. Johan from Denmark came with them. That day Johan became a part of the German speaking group that I walked with in the coming days. I introduced them to my Spanish friends, and we all took a group picture with the Puente la Reina bridge in the background. It was a perfect reunion, and I had another perfect day.

Sharing the burden makes it easier to carry

That day's etapa was from Puente la Reina to Estella (meaning Star). I started early and came to Manjeru in no time. Next was Ciraqui. It stands on a hilltop since Roman times. The view of the town from the distance was fantastic. I was already in Rioja (the famous wine region) and my first view of Ciraqui was through the vineyards. Just as I admired the scenery thre familiar faces came by. Three girls in their late sixties Jozhi, (e)Waldy(ne) and Maya from Nederland. I knew them already from Bayonne. They were on the same evening train to SJPP. So, for the Camino time measures, we knew us for ages.

Jozhi, Waldy and Maya were full of energy, optimism and joy – always ready for jokes and funny things. So, I stopped them and asked if they are for another joke. "Of course, just tell us what to do." I explained to them that all the Americans are here on the Camino because they saw the movie called "The Way" with Charlie Sheen. In that movie there is a scene of main characters walking together through the vineyard here in Rioja. I suggested that we make a movie with the same scene on our own. They were 100% for it. So, we went into the vineyard and became movie stars and film crew. It was fun and we enjoyed it.

Cirauqui was nice but small, so I passed it in minutes. On the way down toward the way the Camino follows an old Roman road, and all the pilgrims cross the bridge which is in one part a ruin of an old Roman bridge. Just beyond that bridge as Camino crosses a modern asphalt road, I met Andrej again. My fellow citizen that I met in Pamplona two days ago at breakfast in Aloha hostel. We spoke just a couple of words since he was waiting for someone that was with him on the Camino and I had to go on.

In Lorca I met Robert. Yesterday we sat together with Tess at the table in Muruzabal. Robert was a big man as tall as me and of the same age. We started to talk, and we walked together toward Estela. We talked and talked, and our conversation got deeper and deeper. I felt he was a soul, I could trust. I told him about my burdens, and I felt a great relief right away. As soon as I shared my burden with him, he took like half of it on his shoulders. It was not much heavier for him, but it was much, much lighter for me. I am still thankful to him that he was such a good listener.

We talked about many, many things and also discussed the people we met on the Camino. One name constantly came in the conversation – Rudi. I didn't know any Rudi, but Rober told me that he was a good friend of his. And shortly after the under-road passage at Villatuerta, just as we started to descend down to the bridge over river Ega, we met the one and only Rudi.

It was my old beard friend from Zubiri. Unfortunately, I didn't know his name until this moment. It was a joyful meeting, and we went on together.

After we crossed a bridge, we met Debi from South Africa. She walked slowly because her knee hurt.

In Estela Robert, Rudi and I agreed we need a beer. So, we went to the main square to find a pub. And there we met the two ladies from Zubir - Jeane and Christine. For them, Rudi and me it was a perfect Zubiri reunion. As we drank beer on the main square my friend Johan from Denmark came along, and we invited him to join us.

Later we had to split since we were all in different hostels. On my way to the Albergue Municipal San Cipriano (hostel is in a sports facility – it shares the showers with the gym) I met two more friends from Zubiri. Bayron and Janete from Canada. We met near the gas station as I was just about to buy some groceries there. I really like these constant meetings – this is one of the greatest things on the Camino. It felt like the whole Zubiri was here in Estella. I started to wonder where Pascal and Helmut might be.

Small towns are keepers of the Holy week magic

Leaving Estela meant leaving my last hostel where I had the reservation that I made back in Zubiri, after good advice from Tess.

I knew I would be in Logroño in two days, the only question was where I would sleep today. My plan was to go all the way to Torres del Rio so it would only be a short distance to walk tomorrow.

This would give me some extra time to stop in Viana and explore one of my must-see points – the grave of Cesare Borgia. The only problem was that the hostel in Torres del Rio was a very small one and I was not able to make a reservation since it was a community hostel. So, I had to hit the road today as early as possible.

I woke up at 5.30 am. and half an hour later I already left the hostel. And just 20 meters from the hostel – practically at the end of its parking I met my German speaking friends. The whole group. Unbelievable. Just yesterday evening I have been wondering where Pascal and Helmut might be and here they were, together with Martin and Johan and a new friend Thomas from Germany. I was delighted to see them all again and to be introduced to Thomas. We went on immediately since they had the same problem. No reservations for the evening. So, it was very important to be in any town, where one intends to sleep, as soon as possible.

Our first stop was the wine fountain Irache. We were there in less than 15 minutes, but it was still closed since it opens only at 7 o'clock. We didn't want to waste time waiting, so we hit on.

We had our breakfast 4 km down the road at Bar Azketako in Azqueta. As we just finished and started to take some photos, German and his friends came and decided to have breakfast here too. I said hello to them and then our German speaking group left for Los Arcos. My friends had a plan to sleep there, and I decided that I will join them and stay at the same hostel as they intend to. So, I said goodbye to my plan to walk all the way to Torres del Rio. It was a good decision since their rhythm was fast, but I got myself a new blister. Fast walking is really not for me. But because of the circumstances – Holy week and no reservation in community hostels – we didn't have any other options.

The etapa from Estela to Los Arcos is a very nice one since you walk through a long wide valley, full of wheat fields that are still green in early spring April.

We came to Los Arcos at midday. We were really early, and it was unbelievable how much time we had that afternoon. First, we went to the Hostel La Casa Austria. They had enough beds for us, but they put us in the garden and called us one by one for check in. As we sat there, we already started to enjoy the afternoon. We got us beers from the vending machine and made a toast to our successful etapa and luck that we had got beds in the hostel.

After we packed our backpacks in the rooms we agreed that supper would be at 5.30 pm. Some of the pilgrims went to rest and three of us went shopping right away. We knew shops would close soon since it was Good Friday.

On our way back from shopping I met my friend Richard again. He was with Coral, Jordi and Albert. I greeted each of them by their names and Coral could not have believed her ears that I had remembered her name. But how could one forget such a nice girl's name. They told me that they are going to Torres del Rio and invited me to come with them. I thanked them for their kind invitation and told them that I was already checked-in in a hostel here in Los Arcos.

After putting groceries in the hostel kitchen, I went sightseeing. Los Arcos has a wonderful church at the main square. An old one and very rich in internal decoration. Definitely a must see. On the main square I saw nervous activity of the locals, who were preparing for the evening procession. It was the Good Friday and everybody, that meant something in this town, had participated. I also saw many pilgrims sitting at the open air tables of the pubs round the main square. A wonderful scene that you can only see in small towns along the Camino. I joined the table where Byron and Janet were sitting and talking with Nelly and Viviana from Switzerland. I also said hello to Jonas, a blonde guy that was already on his second Camino. He had a great Saint James shell tattoo – a tattoo that I started to think about getting one for myself. We sat and talked and waited for the time to pass. All of us waiting for the big evening event.

I went back to my hostel at 4.45 pm. When I came back Helmut and Pascal were already in the kitchen, cooking. Two master chefs of pilgrim meals. Our dinner was great. Made by the pilgrims for the pilgrims. Cooked in a large pot and served to all at the same table. It was a true Camino dinner. I said a prayer and then we ate and talked.

At the table, beside all the men that I walked today with, sat Jana from Germany, Sasha with his daughter Lea (the one I later found on my pictures from the Roncesvalles breakfast), Christine from Maine (USA) and a lady I unfortunately forgot the name of.

Close after 7 pm it was time to go to see the procession. We washed the dishes quickly and went to the main square. Everybody was there. It was packed to the last corner. At 7.30 the procession activities started. It also started to get dark. They had a perfect timing.

We saw the whole procession as it left the main square and again as it passed the junction at the end of our hostel street. It was magnificent. We all enjoyed it very much. The only person that was not amazed was Christina from Maine. On the contrary. She was of African origin and the sight of the procession's characters that looked like Ku Klux Klan members was a big shock for her. We had to calm her down, that all is OK, that this is original Spanish folklore and that it has nothing to do with that part of American history. She survived.

Nox Magna in Logroño

Today we had the same problem as yesterday - no hostel reservation. We also knew that all the people that made it to Torres del Rio yesterday, would be in Logroño today before us.

So, we got up early. Breakfast was quick. Just a coffee and croissant in the pub at Los Arcos main square. And then we started to walk. Walk as fast as possible.

In Torres del Rio I saw Lucia, sitting at the table having her morning coffee. I waved to her and went on. This was the last time I saw that girl with the pearl earrings.

I left Torres del Rio walking with Jana. Jana from Germany had great physical and mental strength. You looked at her and you knew it. She was very well prepared for the Camino and strongly determined to come all the way to Santiago de Compostela. As a person she was smart, kind, modest and always in a good spirit – definitely a very nice person to talk to. She was in the same hostel in Los Arcos and yesterday evening we shared a pilgrims dinner at the same table. So, we already knew each other. I walked with her from Torres del Rio to Viana and we talked a lot. That part of the etapa has lots of ups and downs. Pretty stressful for the legs that are on the Camino already for one week. She walked like it was her first day.

We came to Viana in no time. We were there at 10.45 a.m. I went to see the Cesare Borgia grave and Jana went to get something to eat.

Cesare Borgia was a controversial man – just like his father. According to Wikipedia Cesare was born in Rome in 1475.

He was made Bishop of Pamplona at the age of 15 and archbishop of Valencia at 17. A year later, as his father became Pope Alexander VI on 11th of August 1492, Cesare became cardinal. He was only 18. Six years later on the 17th of August 1498, Cesare became the first person in history to resign the cardinalate. He did it in order to pursue a military career. He was appointed commander general of the papal armies. His fight for power was a major inspiration for "The Prince" by Machiavelli. Cesare Borgia lived in fights and he died in one - her on the outskirts of Viana. Borgia just recaptured Viana, but not the castle, which he then besieged. In the early morning of 11th of March 1507, an enemy party of knights fled from the castle during a heavy storm. Outraged at the ineffectiveness of the siege, Borgia chased them only to find himself on his own. The party of knights, discovering that he was alone, trapped him in an ambush and injured him fatally with a spear. Borgia was originally buried in a marbled mausoleum that John III had ordered to be built at the altar of the Church of Santa María in Viana - one of the stops on the Camino de Santiago. In the 16th century the bishop of Mondoñedo, Antonio de Guevara, wrote about what he had seen being written on the tomb when he had paid a visit to the church. This epitaph underwent several changes in wording throughout the years and the version most commonly cited today is that published by the priest and historian Francisco de Alesón in the 18th century. It reads: "Here lies in a little earth he who everyone feared, he who held in peace and war his hand. Oh, you who go in search of worthy things to praise, if you would praise the worthiest then your path stops here and you do not need to go any farther."

The tomb was destroyed sometime between 1523 and 1608, during which time Santa María was undergoing renovation and expansion. Tradition goes that a bishop of Calahorra considered inappropriate to have the remains of "that degenerate" lying in the church, so the opportunity was taken to tear down the monument and expel Borgia's bones to where they were reburied under the street in front of the church to be trodden on by all who walked through the town. It was a disgrace. In 1945 Borgia was unearthed and his bones were sent to Viana's town hall, directly across from Santa María, where they remained until 1953. They were then reburied immediately outside of the Church of Santa María, no longer under the street. A movement was made in the late 80s to have Borgia dug up once more and put back into Santa María, but this proposal was ultimately rejected by church officials due to recent ruling against the internment of anyone who did not hold the title of pope or cardinal. Since Borgia had renounced the cardinalate, it was decided that it would be inappropriate for his bones to be moved into the church. It was reported that Fernando Sebastián Aguilar, the Archbishop of Pamplona, would acquiesce after more than 50 years of petitions and Borgia would finally be moved back inside the church on 11 March 2007, the day before the 500th anniversary of his death, but an Archbishopric spokesman declared that the church doesn't authorize any such practice. The local church said that "we have nothing against the transfer of his remains. Whatever he may have done in life, he deserves to be forgiven now." Today his remains are still buried under a stone slab in front of the side entrance to the Church of Santa María in Viana.

I stamped my pilgrim's credentials in the church and went on to the main square. There it was already my whole group. Pascal, Helmut, Martin, Johan, Thomas and Jana. She introduced us to her friend Anna from Germany. We had a quick meal out from our backpacks and then we all flew toward Logrono. We only stopped at Maria's street shop since all Germans know HaPe Kerkeling shopped here.

We came to Logrono just before 1 pm and got the last beds in hostel. It was Easter Saturday and Logrono was packed not just with pilgrims but with tourists as well. Logrono is a very popular destination because of it's Easter processions that take place through the whole Holy Week. We agreed to have a pilgrim's dinner, together as a group, just like yesterday. It will be at 6. p.m. I did some laundry first and afterwards I went to explore the town. First, I went to find a place that I knew from a web cam. I wanted to see if the web cam works and if I can make a screenshot of me there. It worked and I did the screen shot. Then I went to a grocery shop to buy some food for the coming days and some desert for today's dinner – I chose strawberries.

As I came back at 5.45 all the men were already in the kitchen preparing our supper and I joined them. Table was ready at 6 pm. After a prayer we started to eat. It was a nice modest pilgrims meal. A one that calms the stomach, warms the heart and fills the soul. After the supper we were ready to go to the Easter vigil that would start at 9 in the Cathedral. As we waited on the main square I met Robert. He explained me the texts on the Cathedral walls. Spain is a nation with lots of history. We that come from outside should respect that and not judge it.

The talk I had with Robert there on the square in front of Logrono Cathedral was our last. It was time for our final Goodbye. I will never forget our walk from Lorca to Estela. He was not a preacher but talking with him was worth thousands of confessions. He was definitely a god's hand that helped to a tortured pilgrim's soul. He took of burden and brought the first sparks of fire to the soul that was on a spiritual journey of a lifetime. As we parted some other *fire* was lit just near by. Easter vigil in the Logrono Cathedral lit a fire and brought light to the darkness that night – to that

dark night – to that big darknes – to that nox magna – to that
Velika noč.

47

Et lux in tenebris lucet. (John 1:5)

Everybody walks the Camino at his's own pace

21st of April 2019 was Easter Sunday. For many Spanish people that I met on the Camino this was the day to travel home. Holy Week was over and so were their holidays. German, Sandra, Marta, Antonio and Juanlu went home. So were Richards friends Lucia, Coral, Albert, Jordi, Aleix, Rosa and Marta. My friend Robert also had to go home. But on the other hand there were other people from Spain that just started the Camino today. In our hostel in Logrono I met Arturo, Angel and Francisco. I will meet them in many of the coming days.

For me Easter Sunday was the beginning of my second week on the Camino. It was a very hard day for me since I was tired from yesterday's running to Logrono. It was so bad that I asked my friends back at home to back me up. They sent me many SMSs, direct messages and mails. It was a great help and I really needed it badly. After seven days of constant daily walking, my body started to show first signs of fatigue. But this was just the beginning. No matter how much you train back at home, you can not prepare yourself for the Camino. You have to take your share of physical suffering here on The Way. It's a part of the Camino experience. And everybody's Camino actually has at least three phases: physical, mental and spiritual.

In the physical phase you fight with your body problems. All the muscle pain, blisters, etc. Many people get injuries that mean the end of their Camino. Twisted ankles. Crashed knees. Some kind of illness with high fever, etc. There are many illnesses and diseases that can happen to a pilgrim. You comprehend that Camino is a very serious project, as you pass many little memorials, for the people that have passed away right there on the Camino. I don't want to scare anybody from doing the Camino. I just want to say it is a serious physical challenge. You will of course be in good hands since Spain's health care system is very well organized. I have seen their medics on the Camino in action. They were there to help a pilgrim in need in less than 15 minutes. The whole Camino is very well covered with a strong telephone and internet signal so you can call 112 at any time.

After the physical phase comes the mental phase as you fight in your head. At a certain moment lots of physical pain and long term fatigue starts to take a mental toll. You start to question the whole project. Unless you are mentally strong and very determined, this can make you quit the Camino. But if you manage to come across this first two phases, you will enter the spiritual phase that will reward you 1000 times for all of your sufferings and take you all the way to Santiago de Compostela - to the field of stars. Camino is definitely: "Per Aspera ad Astra!" ("through hardships to the stars"). We started at 6.30. It was still dark outside as we passed the famous pilgrims monument in Logrono – a young couple with their backpacks. On the other side of the junction we found a pub that was open despite the fact it was Easter Sunday early in the morning. We got our first morning coffee and some French croissants.

The Camino leaves Logrono through two beautiful parks connected with nice modern pedestrian bridges. Just outside the town it comes to a big pond where morning fishermen were already fishing. Here the Camino goes on top of the dam that holds the water of the pond. At the end of the dam we came to something like a picnic place. Around the place there were many rabbits and many rabbit holes. Alice was not there. Neither was there my awareness how deep into the rabbit hole I was destined to go before the end of my Camino.

We were in Navarrete at 10 a.m. There we had our second coffee. On the way there my yesterday blisters got much worse and in the last 3 hours I got another one. I had to treat them right there at the Bocateria Move pub. I also had to do something with the pace of my walking. Our group walked way too fast for me. Fast tempo for the third consecutive day was simply too much for my feet. My blisters were getting worse. I really had to do something.

I decided I will walk at my own pace. A slow walk, but on the other hand I will not stop right after midday, as we did in the last two days. I knew from my past days, that I can do some walking also after lunch, practically through the whole afternoon until dinner time, as I will be finally reaching my daily destination hostel. Such rhythm will become my rhythm for the rest of my Camino - all the way to Santiago de Compostela and Finisterre. Finally, I had to admit that it is true what they say - Everybody walks the Camino at his's own pace. This saying goes off course beyond Spanish Camino, because it is meant also for our life's Caminos.

It is 18km from Navarrete to Nájera. Behind Ventosa the way ascends on a hill and from there you get the first view on Nájera. From there you descend for like 7 km. First the way goes under the asphalt road and then it runs parallel to it. On that way I already had very strong pains in my legs – one part from blisters and one part from tired muscles. It was bad, but I met someone that had it even worse. It was Edita from Germany. Already as I was approaching her, I saw that she must be in a lot of pain. Body Language was telling it all. She would make only one step and stop and then another one and stop again. She must have been in terrible pain. We were somewhere around a big mobile telephone pole that is approximately 5 km from Najera. I stopped and started to talk with her. She was not just physically bad, she was also psychologically bad, because some friends of hers just left her and went on to Nájera. She was totally down. I told her I will not leave her and promised her I will escort her all the way to Nájera. This would of course some how jeopardize my today's plan to go all the way to Azofra but this didn't matter at the moment. Pilgrim in need was my priority. I told her I am in pain too but assured her that we can both do it to Nájera. I offered her my walking poles which she gratefully accepted.

So, I talked and talked to her and asked her a lot of questions. And we proceed slowly. After a while I saw she is getting better. She was still in much pain, but she started to get in a much better mood. I was glad. After more than an hour of slow walking and a lot of talking we came to the outskirts of Nájera. And at the first pub there, the two friends of hers have been waiting for her. She thanked me for not letting her alone and returned me the poles. We took a photo together and I went on. In a couple of minutes, I was at the bridge over river Najerilla. There I met some local ladies that wanted to see my pilgrim's stick. After we took some pictures, I had to call my friends that were already in some hostel here in Nájera. After a while I got Pascal, and he gave me the directions. At that moment Edita came along. She was much better.

My friend was in Albergue de Peregrinos Municipal de Nájera. It was not just the whole German speaking group but also my old friend Richard. We haven't seen each other for 2 days. The last time we met was in Los Arcos and he and his friends were on their way to Torres del Rio. Now he was alone. His friends have gone home. My friends were already all checked in and they all invited me to join them in the hostel. I explained to them that today I have done a lot of thinking about my pace on the Camino and that I have reached the conclusion that I will walk slowly but make a larger distance every day. Long distances were a must for me since my plan was to come to Santiago de Compostela on Tuesday, May 14th and fly back home the next day. I knew I had to be home by Friday, since on Saturday the 18th of May, one of my best friends had his 50th birthday party. What I haven't explained to my friends was that I also have a secret wish. To go to Finisterra as well. But for that I needed 3 extra days. That afternoon in Nájera Finistera was still nothing more than a wish. My friends were sad that I would leave the group, so it was a little bit of a sad goodbye. But since I was a slow walker and since I started to walk later than they did, we would still be meeting each other on the Camino in the next couple of days. Martin was the last one I said goodbye before I left for Azofra. He was a really good man.

And he was really sad that I am leaving. I was sad too. I knew I would miss them all, but I had to. I have decided for my pace. The pace that would be more gentle to my feet and the one that would bring me to Santiago de Compostela according to my plan. I knew it, there was no other option - it was my Camino and I had to walk it alone. After all, it was not the first time that I would walk in my life completely alone. It was my choice.

As I reached Azofra at the end of that day I thanked my family and friends for all the support. I really needed it.

My hardest day

55

Monday 22nd of April was the hardest day of my Camino. I woke up at 7 a.m and as I managed to sit up on the rim of my bed, I was not sure if I could stand up, let alone walk for another whole day. After 8 days of walking my feet were devastated. That morning I was a total ruin.

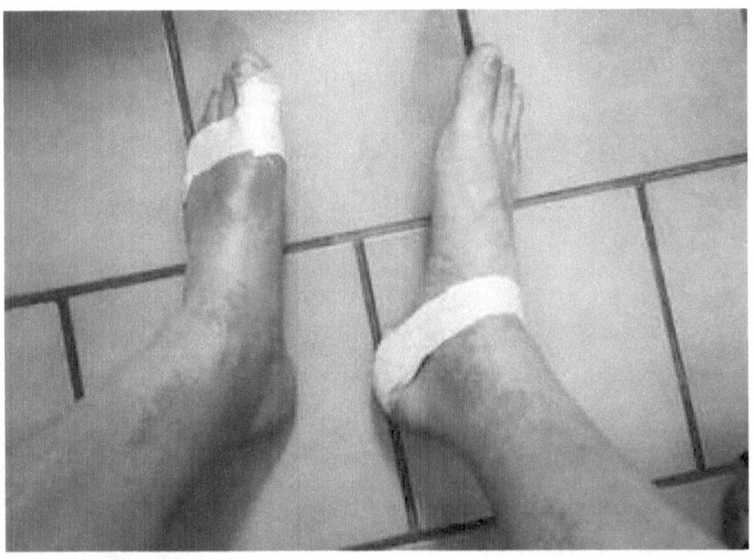

But I had to go to the toilet. After a while I managed somehow to pool together all my strength and I stood up. I made a first step, and then another. Toilets were luckily just around the corner - just like some 10 steps away. I made those 10 steps. And then I made 10 steps back. I made my first 20 steps of that day. I knew I can do it.

I took the next half an hour to take care of my blisters. First Compeed patches and than adhesive tape to fix them. Then I pulled on my socks. And then I firmly tied the laces on my shoes. That did the job. I was kind of ready to walk.

First steps hurt like hell, but by the time I came to Ciriñuela I was already OK. I got myself a decent breakfast at Bar Jacobeo and then I went on. On the way, just some half kilometre from Ciriñuela, I got one of my favourite pictures from the Camino – me in a yellow windbreaker and a matching colour field behind me.

It was one of my first photos of the Camino's landscape vastness. Many more will come in the days on the Meseta. That picture made my day and the food I ate started to boost my muscles with energy. It felt great so I kicked in and started to walk faster.

Just after the ascent through the fields turns to descend toward Santo Domingo de la Calzada I met Jana. I was really happy to see her again. We walked and talked all the way down to the town. Then we had split since I had to go to the pharmacy. Santo Domingo de la Calzada was the last big town before Burgos. And Burgos was two and a half days of walking away. And I knew I needed to do some blister treatment stocks.

After Pharmacy I went to a grocery store and then to Planeta Agua where I bought a new pair of walking socks. After the ATM visit I was ready for all the challenges on the way to Burgos. But first I had to visit the famous church. There, for more than 1000 years, pilgrims have been visiting the grave of Santo Domingo. The legend goes that he has saved a young man's life. That young man was a pilgrim and he was falsely charged that he had stolen something valuable from the noble house where he spent the night. It was actually the daughter of the house lord, who put that valuable thing in a young man's bag as revenge for his rejection. The man was hanged the next morning, but Santo Domingo saved him. At midday people came to the local sheriff to tell him that the young man was alive. He was just about to have lunch and didn't want to be disturbed. So he said that this is not possible and that by then, the man must be as dead as the roasted rooster on his plate. And at that moment the rooster stood up from the plate and started crowing. In memory of that miracle, you can still see the live roosters in the church, just above the saint's grave.

On the plaza in front of the church I met my German speaking group again. We went to the entrance of the church. Some of us went inside and some stayed outside, to look after our backpacks. I prayed on the grave of the saint to take us safely to Santiago de Compostela. Helmut showed us how to provoke the rooster above the grave to crow. One just has to mimic the crow sound and the rooster responds.

As we returned from the church Anna was doing some yoga stretching. I guess her legs hurt but she was in a good mood as always – a true sunshine flower. Her tattoo really mirrored her character.

Beside Pascal, Helmut, Martin, Thomas, Jana, Anna, Sascha and his daughter Lea, I also met Arturo. He and his friends Angel and Francisco were in the same hostel in Logrono. We said hello and took a picture together. Later I asked my German friends what their plans were. They planned to go eat something here in Santo Domingo de la Calzada and then to go to their hostel in Grañón.

My plan was to go to Viloria de Rioja where I made a reservation at the famous hostel: Refugio Acacio & Orietta. I would like to join my friends for lunch but I still had quite some distance to walk. So I said farewell to my friends and went on. Some of them I saw for the last time. I will meet again with Martin, Helmut, Thomas and Jana. But with Pascal, Anna, Sascha and Lea I had my last goodbye. The last one I said goodbye to was little Lea. She held my pilgrim stick as I took pictures with Arturo. She was little but strong. I was amazed that such a little girl could walk so much. I envied her father that he was blessed to have his daughter as a companion on the Camino. I hope someday at least one of my three daughters will do the Camino with me. Only God knows when, if ever.

I came to Grañón at 4 p.m. I was on my feet practically the whole day and my feet were very bad already in the morning. Now it was not just the feet. The problem was that I was exhausted. But I had to go on so I turned on some music to cheer me up and give me some strength.

I crossed the border to Leon and at 5.30 I was in Redecilla del Camino. I broke down on a bench. I had to rest. I had to eat. And I desperately needed as much mental strength as possible.

Already back at home my friend Vrti told me that such moments would come. So I was prepared. I started to listen to the speech by US Admiral McRaven. It is one of the best motivational speeches. A speech that even today still gives me goosebumps. A perfect motivation speech for a lonely pilgrim at the end of his strength.

I listened to the speech and ate the last pieces of bread from my backpack. Right then Marion from Germany passed me with her bicycle. She waved and I waved her back. Only later, as we were eating dinner at the hostel, she told me how ruined I looked there on the bench in Redecilla del Camino. At that moment neither of us knew that we would be at the same hostel. If I did know that, I would have asked her to tell our hosteleros that I would be late. I was only 4 kilometers from my hostel but I would still need another hour and a half to get there. Those 4 kilometers would be the hardest 4 kilometers on my whole Camino.

McRaven's speech lifted my spirit but I was physically still totally down. But after such a speech I didn't want to quit. I was not a loser. I was a fighter and quitting was not an option. So I stood up. I put on my backpack. I prepared my walking poles. I took the rosary out of my pocket, said a prayer, and hung it around my neck. I put the earphones in my ears and I set the music on my phone to only one song - Natural (by Imagine Dragons). I started to walk and those constant "You hold the line when ewery one is giving up or giving in ... You're standing on the edge, face up ... Took an oath by the blood of my hand. I swear, I'M GONNA MAKE IT!" did their job. They took me to Viloria de Rioja.

It took me a lot of self motivation, an unprecedented stubrenes and an iron will to do those last kilometers. It was really hard but I did it. I was so proud of myself.

And I was so happy I was finally at Refugio Acacio and Orietta. But seniora Orietta was not. I was so late and I have not let her know I will be late. Seniora was cooking dinner and she was not sure if it was going to be enough for everyone since I was a late show up. She gave me a speech and I was given only 15 minutes to shower and to sit down at the table. Here it is tradition that all the pilgrims sit and eat together with Acacio and Orietta. They tell their story and then every pilgrim tells his or her story. Acacio is from Brazil and Orietta is from Italy. They met on the Camino and fell in love. Later they married and decided they will work in the Camino hostels. They did that for years and as they got enough money they opened one on their own.

Beside them at the table I met Claudia and Edita (mother and daughter) from Switzerland, a couple from Italy, Julijon from France and Marion from Germany. It was one of the most beautiful dinner experiences on the Camino. They knew their business. Acacio is a great host and seniora Orietta is a great cook. Her dinner was delicious. And it was enough for everyone so she relaxed. After dinner, as she already knew how hard my day was, she came and apologized to me for her speech. I said it was OK, that I should have called and let them know I would be late.

Acacio and Orietta are great people. And their story is one of many Camino stories. I like stories. And I have heard many on the Camino. Some of them I wrote myself. It is actually people and their stories that make pilgrims come back to the Camino - again and again and again …

Everybody respects if you want to walk alone

I had a great breakfast at Acacio and Orietta and started my walk at 8.30. Immediately as I exited the hostel it came all clear to me why I had such a hard day yesterday. Weather got bad today. Me being a weather sensitive person must have felt the influence already yesterday in the afternoon. That combined with 9 consecutive days of walking explained everything.

Today I was OK. I was on the road, and I was alone. Half an hour later Marion from Germany passed me with her bike. She waved goodbye and this was the last time I saw her. At 11am I was in Belorado. Right away, as you enter the town, there is an albergue on the right side of the way called "A Santiago". There I met Martin. He was alone. The rest of the German speaking friends were nowhere to see. So, I asked him where the others are? He explained to me that today he wanted to walk alone.

This was one of the things that impressed me on the Camino, how respectful pilgrims are for such wishes. It is basically some kind of Camino law that people respect your wishes for solitude if you express one. Everybody understands that there are certain moments when a pilgrim needs to be alone with his own thoughts.

I understood that too, so we wished each other Buen Camino. He went inside for breakfast, and I went on. At the main square I saw another familiar face. It was Edita from Germany. She came to Belorado by bus. Her injury was not much better, so she skipped a day. She was not sure how she would continue. We parted with a common Buen

Camino. Sadly, I have not seen her again. I hope she made it to Santiago.

As I exited Belorado it started to rain. I put on all my rain gears and continued to walk. It was actually my first real rain on the Camino. The first one I had was only a spray of water on the top of the Pyrenees on Palm Sunday 9 days ago.

In Tosantos at 1pm the weather was still pretty bad, and it was not much better at 2pm in Villambistia. An old Camino sign with San Esteban church as a background made one of my favorite photos of the day and the village fountain was a great symbol of today's weather. *water, water, water*.

From Espinosa del Camino you can already catch the first glimpse of the Villafranca Montes de Oca. Villafranca being the place, Pascal told me in ourair

 phone conversation, they will spend the night. But my destination was still much further. Today I will sleep in a monastery.

Villafranca Montes de Oca was the first of many Villafrancas I would pass. No surprise since I was on the French Camino and in the past people from France have set many settlements along this way. Town lies at the mouth of a valley and behind the town rises the mountains that gave the town part of its name. Directly from the main town road the Camino starts to ascend into the mountains. I left Villafranca Montes de Oca at 4pm.

In late April, nature in Montes de Oca was still in winter sleep. Just Primroses - first signs of the coming spring – only started to pop out. And as I started to ascend the temperature started to drop. It was rainy and it was cold. For the next 4 hours I would walk through the mountain woods.

I have had an outer raincoat that has covered me and my backpack. It was just a simple yellow plastic foil with two or three buttons in front. It turned out that its quality was strongly correlated with its price. It was a cheap product. I paid it only 9,99 euros. And after many hours of walking it was torn to pieces. I tried to knot it together somehow but it ripped again. Fortunately, just shortly after I left Villafranca it stopped raining so I threw it in the litter bin at the first pilgrim stop on my way up the Oca mountains.

For the rest of the afternoon the walk was nice. In the evening even some sun came through the clouds and some blue sky showed in the south. At 8pm I finally came to Monasterio San Juan de Ortega.

Ortega means Nettles as there were plenty around the place as San Juan started to build the monastery in 1142. San Juan is buried in the Church he started to build. The church of St. Nicholas is named after San Nicolas de Bari who saved his life by calming the sea as he was returning from his trip to the Holy Land; a journey he took shortly after his teacher Santo Domingo's death. Prayers at San Juan de Ortega's grave became famous in Spanish history as Spanish queen Isabella la Catolica prayed here in the 15th century. San Juan de Ortega is the patron to all women that want to become blessed with a child.

After Santo Domingo de la Calzada this was my second chance to pray at the grave of the saint. After a prayer I entered the monastery and got a bed. Unfortunately, I was too late for dinner, so I just had a snack from my backpack. I was also too late to do the laundry. Luckily, I still had one clean set of underwear and a clean T-shirt. But laundering my clothes moved up to the top of my priorities for the next day. The bed and the room were OK. After 10 days you also get used to the smell, even if it is potentiated with the humidity of rain-soaked clothes and shoes. I took a shower, and as I laid down in my upper bed, sleep came in no time.

Snow made the coldest day

Wednesday was rainy, snowy and windy. It started pretty normal. Just a cloudy mountain morning. But already after the first hour as I was on the top of another mountain, from which I had a view down on Ages, the rain was already pouring, and the wind was strong. So, as I came down to the town I entered the first inn to warm me up and to have breakfast. I remember the millstone in front of the inn and a little sign that said 518 kilometers to Santiago de Compostela.

After the good morning meal I went on to Atapuerca. It was still raining and it started to get colder. All of a sudden it started to snow. OMG I never expected to have snow on the Camino. That is why I chose to walk in April and May. But here I was - walking the Camino in snow. This was definitely my worst weather day on the Camino. And it has only just begun.

Shortly after Atapuerca the Camino ascends on a hill. It goes along a barbed wire fence where it used to be a military territory. Today the only function of the barbed wire is to comb the sheeps. You can see a lot of wool caught in the fence. As I ascended up the slope it stopped snowing, but as I came to the Cruz de Atapuerca, at the top of the hill, it was still a good moment to say a prayer for better weather for the rest of the Camino days. I guess I was heard, but for today it was still some penance to be done.

Not far from the cross is a pilgrim's monument – a sign that reads: "Since the pilgrim dominated the mountains of Navarra Burguete and saw the areas of Spain spread out before him, he has not enjoyed more beautiful views than this."

The wind got stronger on the other side of the hill. In my opinion it got up to a stormy level and the only way, out of this storm, was down toward Rio Pico valley.

As I walked through Cardenuela and Orbaneja, the valley really offered good wind protection. Orbaneja is just a shot away from the Burgos Airport. Camino there goes along its outer fence. All of the sudden you realize you are coming to a suburban landscape of a modern-day town. It tears you out of all your medieval romantic thoughts that have been fed for the last couple of days in Santo Domingo de la Calzada, in Reliegos, in Villafranca Montes de Oca and and especially in the monasterio of San Juan de Ortega.

After a long loop around the airport the road crosses a railway and less than 100m later it comes perpendicular to the main Burgos avenue – Calle Vitoria. This side of Burgos is an industrial suburb with big truck parkings and large warehouses. I crossed the avenue and entered a small truckers inn called – Cafeteria Buenos Aires. I was cold and I was hungry. I sat down at the table where two other pilgrims were already sitting. One of them was Jan from Sweden. I will meet him many times in the coming days.

The meal warmed me up and so did the furnace that stood at the wall near our table. We talked about the bad weather and the waitress told us it was no surprise to them. Burgos tends to be a town famous for strong winters and on the other hand very pleasant, not too hot, in summer. Although it was nice to hear that there are places in Spain that are not furnaces in the summer, especially as you hear all the "hot" stories from the summer Meseta, it did not give me much comfort, since outside it was still windy and cold.

I left the warm furnace of a Good-air cafe at 4pm. I had to go on. It was a bad decision since it got me into one of today's last and worst rain showers. It rained like cats and dogs. And there was no shelter on this part of Calle Victoria. All of the sudden I felt my rain gear trousers were no longer able to hold up and water started to pour through the fabric, then down my legs and – yikes – into my shoes. Damn it! Wet shoes are a walker's nightmare. A perfect condition for a blister disaster.

I swam in my shoes and I shivered of cold. I was desperad again. I had to think and act quickly. But Calle Victoria is a long street. And You are really a winner as you finally came to the road sign reading Burgos. You are finally in town.

Already as I was walking the Victoria I googled all the sport shops in town. It was more than clear to me I needed new rain trousers and definitely, absolutely, unconditionally, immediately … some thermal underwear. I was as cold as the North Pole.

The first sports shop was luckily on Victoria. I got the underwear. I tried it. It fitted me and I didn't took it of for the rest of the day. Rain trousers – the real Gore Tex once – were more of a challenge. Here in Sports Outlet Manzanedo they had only one pair of trousers that barely fitted me, it was also a very simple one and it was also not at a very outlet price. So I only bought thermal underwear and went on to see the other sports shops.

But first I had to come to the centre and I had to get a bed and a place to leave my backpack. I got a bed in the hostel on Calle San Juan vis a vis Hotel Jacobeo. I have shared it with two pilgrims that were on the Camino with their bicycles. Luckily they came to the room earlier and managed to dry most of their clothes on the large radiator in our room. So I got practically the whole radiator for myself.

In the meantime the rain stopped. I put on my sandals and started to run around the town to get the proper pair of rain trousers. Summit Mountain Sports and nature sounded very promising but the problem was my height. They were well stocked but unfortunately did not have the number large enough for me. I am 6'5" (195 cm) and it looks like they do not have many customers of such size in sport shops in Burgos since it was the same story at Solorunners at Avenida de la Paz. At the end I had to go all the way back to Sports Outlet Manzanedo and take what was the only barely fitting pair of GoreTex trousers in town. No matter the design and price.

This shopping didn't cost me just money but also another couple of kilometres of walking. Well at least without my backpack. And it also cost me time. I still wanted to see the famous cathedral but the daylight of the day was already fading out. So I had to run there.

As I came to the plaza in front of the church I was surprised with the scene of my German speaking friends just making the group picture. It was a great joy to be reunited again. Warm hugs and lots of laughing. I joined them for the picture and they explained to me what a tough walk they had today since they started in Villafranca Montes de Oca and so having 4 more hours of walking to Burgos as myself. They were also all wet and frozen through the day, but now we were all great.

Unfortunately I couldn't join them for a mug of beer, since I had to catch the laundry that was open only until 10pm. I got there in time but the lady that came to lock the facility had to wait for an extra 10 minutes for all my laundry to tumble dry completely.

With my underwear freshly washed and with my new thermal gears and Gore Tex trousers I was ready for the Meseta.

Fascinating vastness of the Meseta

I got up at 8 am and managed to tape all the blisters by 8.45 am. All wet clothes dried up over the night and most importantly - the shoes were dry too. It was really a small miracle. Without such a strong heating radiator it would be impossible to dry the shoes literally overnight. I was really happy about that.

I checked out at 9.15 and took the last picture with the famous Burgos cathedral at 9:30. There I met a pilgrim from a neighbouring country – Croatia. He was the only Croatian I met on the Camino. He was on the Camino with a group of friends from Bavaria, Germany, where he lives and works.

Camino gets out of Burgos through more pleasant parts of the town than it enters. No industrial suburbs, but more city parks and green alleys. After you exit the town, you come to a challenge of navigating the labyrinth roads that take you on the other side of the highway, but even there the friendly Spanish people left some great notes of encouragement for the pilgrims. Highway company apologizes for the inconvenience of navigating the Camino around and under the highway and some street artists have made great Camino graffiti on the pillars of the highway viaducts.

The weather today was windy, and the wind brought rain showers practically every hour. But I was warm and dry. The new equipment was doing a great job.

Shortly after this maze I came to Tardajos where I took a break for breakfast at Restaurante Pececitos. A great warm tortilla, freshly squeezed orange juice and a cup of coffee con leche.

One kilometre later comes Rabe de las Calzadas and beyond this town you ascend through a short valley on the famous Meseta. The views on Meseta are magnificent. Meseta conquers your heart immediately. After all the days you have spent until now more or less in ups and downs on the mountains and hills of Navara, Roja, and Montes de Oca, you are finally out on the plain. And it is as plain as possible. This eastern part of the Meseta is a high plateau. Only now and then a valley meanders through it. Wherever your sight reaches it is only a plain green field. Yes, in April it is still all green. Wheat, Barley and Rye. And in the middle of those fields, it is only one tree.

I guess it is one of the most photographed trees on the Camino. From now on trees are going to be a scarce commodity. No problem in April or May but pilgrims really miss their shadows on hot summer days.

First hours on the Meseta were pure joy. It is really hard to describe in words how impressed I was. I have to admit that I was a little bit tired and that my progress was slower than in recent days. I guess that yesterday's storms and afternoon rain gear chasing have left their mark on my body and soul, but as soon as I saw that magical plain, all the wind power plant fields, all the green fields and all the clouds flying above over the plain, I become enchanted and I forgot all my fatigues. My friend back at home that followed my posts noticed a change in my mood and commented that they could see that now I really started to enjoy the Camino.

I guess this day was the turning point in my physical condition. Blisters were still there but they were under control and not as painful as 5 days ago. They will get better and better every day. In just 3 days from now I will stop using bandages. Skin on my feet will get hard enough to do the job on it's own. All the blisters and the muscle pain are going to become just a memory. So today it was the beginning of a farewell to the physical pain - to all muscles pain and all the blisters. I was over the worst physical part. I was exiting the physical phase of my Camino.

But there with all the excitement of entering the Meseta I didn't know that after the physical phase comes the mental phase. A phase where you do not fight with your body, but in your head. But right there shortly after Rabe de las Calzadas all this was still miles and days away. At that moment I felt like I was on the top of the world. It was mid-afternoon. I did 2/3 of today's walking and I was about to see one of the most beautiful views on the Camino – the view over Hornillos del Camino.

I got to the point where Camino starts to descend toward Hornillos del Camino at 3.40pm. The view is really magnificent. No wonder it was caught on cameras and posted so many times. It is one of the most beautiful sceneries on the Camino.

At Hornillos del Camino I took another break. I had to eat. I guess I have already burned all the calories of the late breakfast tortilla. I ordered a hot broth with beans, and it tasted great. By now I already figured it out, that eating meat for breakfast or lunch is not such a good idea. Digestion of proteins simply takes too much of energy, energy that you actually need for walking. By now I also knew that I have a different rhythm than most of the pilgrims. I was a slow walker, but I could walk all day. I just needed a couple of breaks where I have to eat.

It was 5 pm as I left Hornillos del Camino. It was up out of the valley and on the Meseta again. I was alone. No more pilgrims on the road. Most of them decided to stay back in Hornillos del Camino. There are some very nice hostels there, but my goal was to walk another 7,5 miles (12 kilometres) to Hontanas.

I enjoyed the high plateau views again. I was halfway between Hornillos del Camino and Hontanas around 7 pm as I saw a storm approaching. Dark clouds were coming from the horizon with unbelievable speed. It was the high wind that runs over the Meseta.

I was at the rim of the small waley named San Bol. I stopped and took out of my backpack all the rain gear again. It took me 5 minutes to dress and to cover the backpack with the rain protection membrane. Then I had to run into the valley. At a small junction on the bottom of the valley first drops of rain started to fall. I wanted to run another 100m down the road on the left side, to the house that I had seen, but I was too late. In no time the storm was on me. There was just a little sign board at the junction, and I managed to reach it in the last seconds before the storm struck with total force.

It was a storm I have not seen in my life. I pressed my body to the board, and I felt how the wood on the other side was flogged with the force of rain driven by the stormy wind. I was like the devil itself had come to chase the clouds across the land. Wind was so strong that, as I looked around from my tiny shelter, I saw that rain drops flew horizontally. I did not know how this was going to end so I said a prayer. It crossed my mind it could well be my last. I guess it would be my last one if this hell had got me up on the plane. I remembered a quote from Murakami's book Kafka on the Shore: "And once the storm is over, you won't remember how you made it through, how you managed to survive. You won't even be sure whether the storm is really over. But one thing is certain. When you come out of the storm, you won't be the same person who walked in. That's what this storm's all about."

This storm was a great metaphor for my whole pilgrimage. Camino was one of the hardest challenges in my life and I was not the same person when I came back home. *Elements* transformed me.

Storm lasted for half an hour and the sign board that gave me shelter had endured it. So was I. Toward the end, as it all started to calm down, I realised that such storms are the reason why all the villages are in the valleys. It is the only way to protect them. Up on the plain they would be blown away in no time.

Rain stopped so suddenly as it started. Ten minutes after the rain stopped the storm was already far away on the horizon – somewhere beyond Hornillos del Camino and Rabe de las Calzadas.

I left San Bol valley at 7:30 pm. Fifteen minutes later a car came and stopped 20 meters behind me on the road. A lady stepped out and took a picture of me. I guess during the storm she might have been at that house, 100 meters down the road in San Bol valey, and had observed me struggling with the forceful storm behind that little sign board. I wonder what thoughts went through her head? I guess I will never know because as she sat back in her car and drove past me she did not stop and we didn't speak a word.

I came to Hontanas at 8.40 pm and got a bed at Hostel Juan de Yepes. I got the last bed in a large room at the end of the corridor. Julion from France that I met at Acacio and Orietta was there. It was nice to see him again. Gabriel and his father were from Brazil and a husband and his wife were from Argentina. All four were on the Camino with their bikes and they came to Santiago de Compostela a week later. In the room there were also two girls. One from Finland and the other one from Czechia. They were shy and didn't talk much.

The hostel looked great as it has been renovated only recently. After the shower I went to the restaurant and had a delicious supper. Eggs with a lot of prosciutto, bread (and a large beer) meant a lot of protein for my muscles to recuperate over the night.

The most beautiful view of the Camino

I had a strong breakfast with bread and butter with marmalade, yoghurt, orange juice and a cup of coffee. At breakfast I met the bikers from South America. We took a picture on the terrace of the restaurant. I started to walk at 9. From Hontanas the Camino follows a small valley all the way to an old monastery of Saint Anton. Julion caught me just shortly before I got there. Monastery of Saint Anton is a well-preserved ruin and as the road passes under old arches you can still see small niches in the walls where the monks have left the bread for the lonely and hungry pilgrims that have passed the monastery through the centuries on their way to Santiago de Compostela.

Today you can stop for a meal just a little bit further down the road on the right side in a small garden inside the monastery walls. A friendly gentleman holds a restaurant there and we decided to stop for a cup of coffee. Julion sat down and I went to the bar to order. There at the bar were already a father and son from the USA.

As I answered the bartender's question about where I came from, they were surprised to find out that I am from the same country as their first lady. And as the bartender showed us that there is the Slovenian flag on his wall, we had to take a picture together. Julion took a great photo. Unfortunately, I forgot the names of the two gentlemen, but I highly respect them for all the credit they gave to Melania and Donald Trump. Something that you unfortunately don't hear very often. I also found their idea of a father & son Camino very nice.

As we left the Saint Anton monastery ruins, I already saw the magnificent hilltop castle of Castrojeriz. From the name I assume that this hill had a strategic position already in the Roman times (castrum – lat. meaning castle). The road from Saint Anton to Castrojeriz is a mile long straight line and I stopped many times to take pictures of the castrum hill and the church at its foots. The views were really magnificent. Taking so much time for photos costed me to stay behind and lost Julion. He was also a much faster walker than I am.

I haven't stopped in Castrojeriz since I already stopped at Saint Anthony's monastery. Behind Castrojeriz Camino crosses a broad river valley over a long stone bridge with many arches that was built by Romans. After crossing the Rio Odra Camino ascends the steep hill slopes of Alto de Mostelares. It is a pretty tough ascend but the macadam road is broad and well maintained.

On the top I took a break and had a snack and drink from my backpack. I rested and enjoyed the view. The view back on the Castrojeriz and Rio Odra valley is magnificent. But it is nothing to what Camino brought me just a couple of hundred yards later. I TO THE MOST BEAUTIFUL POINT ON THE CAMINO.

I saw it on many posts from the Camino, but to see it in real, with my own eyes, was beyond all expectations. I was there. In my dreams. It was magical.

Two years before I started my Camino I found a picture of that view on the internet and it became my motivational picture through all my preparational trainings for the Camino.

I started to train physically already back in January – running for 10 km three times a week and later, from late February on, I changed the weekend run to mountaineering, to prepare myself also for the Pyrenees crossing. That picture has kept me motivated through all of my trainings. And now here I was. At this very same spot. Unbelievable. I was totally impressed. It is a view I would really like everybody to have a chance to see at least once in a lifetime. It is so magnificent. The Meseta lays under your feet and the fields are stretching all the way to the horizon. No boundaries. No limitations. Endless. Free.

After my dream came true, I had to pull myself together and go on. Beyond the horizon I came to a small hostel at the stone bridge over river Pisuerga. It is called Hospital de Peregrinos San Nicolas de Puente Litero (Puente = bridge, litero = stone). It is one of the most authentic hotels. I would like to stay there but today I wanted to come all the way to

Fromista. So, I just had a coffee with the hospitaliero and took a look at the interior.

Hostal used to be a church. Inside in the main nave is a long table for the joint meals and at its back and up on the chorus lies the beds for the pilgrims. Very modest and very traditional.

As I crossed rio Pisuerga I was already in the next province – in Palencia. First village was Itero de la Vega where I met many familiar faces in front of the local hostels and restaurants. One of them was Julion. He has not checked in yet, so he made the decision to join me on my way to Fromista.

Walking with him for a while gave me the opportunity to learn that this is his second Camino and that it is his intention to do it differently as the first one. This time he is doing it in a more modest and more spiritual way. He was really very humble and pulled back. A great soul to walk with. His intention was to go all the way to Finistere and to take a week of rest there. He has told me that there in Finistere, the rule that you can stay in the hostel just for one night does not apply, so you can stay as long as you like.

I told him that I have this dream too, to go to Finistere, but currently my time constraints do not give me the freedom to go there. My schedule at that time was to come to Santiago de Compostela on Tuesday the 14th of May and to fly back home the next day. I had to be home before Saturday 18th of May since my friend is having his 50th birthday celebration. So going Extra 90 kilometres through Wednesday, Thursday and Friday and returning home on Saturday all the way from Finistere, over Santiago de Compostela and Venice airports and shuttle from Venice to Slovenia and to come directly to the party was no option.

Totally out of the question. I told Julion that it would only be doable if I manage to do some extra-long walks on the Meseta plain and get in some extra days. Today's 34 kilometres from Hontanas to Fromista are a great start to that option. They are showing that on the Meseta it is possible to walk more than 30 kilometres in a day. That is something that was impossible on the etapas that went over the mountains and hills up until now. Today's distance also shows that my physical condition is getting great and that I am really pass all the blisters and muscle pain. At that moment this tiny little dream suddenly started to look doable and in the next few days it would grow and motivate me from within to make it come true. To go all the way to Santiago de Compostela and to the end of the world. But It would take a lot of physical effort and a great mental toll. It would also call for all the luck and all the guarding **angels** to protect me from all the possible injuries, diseases, and other pilgrims' misfortunes.

Last miles before Camino reaches Fromista are along the irrigation channel. There it feels like the Netherlands. There are even some boats in the water canal. The canal ends at water locks in Fromista which are a monument of technical heritage and are not operating anymore. Today they are one of Fromistas tourist attractions. For me they were also important because of the tourist biro that stands near them. This tourist biro has a high quality web camera overlooking the water locks. This was the second camera I had on my list (first one was in Logrono).

I told Julion about the camera and we both called our families to turn on the computers and go to the camera's web page. It was nice to talk to my girls back at home and they were delighted to see me on Fromista's web camera. I talked a long while with them, I waved to them, walked around the water locks and they commented and asked many questions about my Camino so far. As I finished my phone call, I lost Julion again. This time for good.

In Fromista I went to the church first. They had a great celebration, so it was packed with people. I noticed that it must have been renovated recently. I especially liked the new wooden floor. I do not see such floors in our churches, but I noticed it as a kind of trend in Spain. In contrast to stone it gives a great warm impression to the interior of the church.

I left the church just before 7pm because I had to find a bed. I got it in the last hostel at the end of the street since all the others were full. Looks like the church festivities have attracted many people to Fromista.

Meeting Paul

Saturday was my third day on the Meseta. I was now deep into its heartland. Here you can see the next town from the very moment after you have left the previous one. Meseta is that flat.

Saturday started with a sunny morning, and I was in a good mood after a strong breakfast in a small canteen in Fromista. The town was very peaceful in the morning. Looks like the celebrations went long into the night and people were still enjoying a good morning sleep.

I passed the Poblacion de Campos and Revenga de Campos before midday and stopped in Villarmentero de Campos for lunch. I have entered the garden of Albergue Amanecer. It is a great garden where you are not alone since owners' hens would always give you company. I ordered a paella and sat down at one of the tables with hens.

At that very moment I saw a big man entering the garden looking where to sit down. Sometimes even before the person speaks, its energy speaks for himself. And this man's energy was low. Very low. I saw that he was in a really bad condition.

He looked very, very tired. And he was alone. Since my only company were chickens, I waved to him to come and join me at my table.

We introduced ourselves and he sat down. His name was Paul and he was a pilgrim from the USA. I asked him what is going on with him and he explained that he feels extremely exhausted. He has also caught a cold, due to the bad weather of the recent days. He might even have had a fever in the morning but he thought the fever had gone away by now.

He said that he is in a terrible mood today and that he thinks he is going to take a taxi for his afternoon etapa.

I told him not to do that because at the end of his pilgrimage he will be sorry that he has not walked the whole Camion. I knew that he wanted, just like me, to do the whole thing the old way - on foot. He definitely didn't look like the kind of pilgrims that use all kinds of transportations to do the etapas or post service to deliver their backpack. His shoes, trousers and backpack showed that he was on the road. Going through the same rain and muddy roads as I was. If I understand him correctly he was an ex soldier. So he was used to fighting. He just needed a little bit of motivation.

So I asked him »How many years did it take you to come to the Camino? How many years have you dreamed to finally get a chance to walk this ancient pilgrimage way?«

Paul: »I wanted to do it for years, but never found the time.«

Me: »And now you are here. Can you imagine how many people would want to be here in your place?«

Paul: »I guess many. You are right there are many people who can still only dream to be here someday.«

Me: »So you see. We are actually lucky ones to be here.«

Paul: »Yes we are. I guess we should be kind of thankful to be here?«

Me: »Yes, we should.«

Paul: »So we should actually not complain about anything here?«

Me: »We should not. We should only be thankful for the opportunity to be here and to walk this Camino as we have dreamed for a long time. «

»You are right. There are many people that are not as happy as we are. Who would really want to be here on the Camino, but can't. And we are here and we walk the Camino. We are really the lucky ones«, Paul concluded.

We talked for an hour about the Camino and we ate our lunch. Through this conversation his energy transformed. As we finished our lunch he was in a much, much better mood. The talk and the food did their job. He was smiling and he was determined to do the rest of this etapa on foot. The taxi idea was only a bad moment in history. I was glad he felt so uplifted.

As we parted he said: »Jorg ,you cannot imagine how much it meant to me that you invited me to your table.«

»Paul, as I saw you, I noticed right away that you need someone to talk to. I am glad you are now much better. I hope we meet again. Buen Camino!«

»Buen Camino!«

My next stop was in Villalcazar de Sirga where I visited their beautiful church and took a picture with the famous statue of the pilgrim sitting at the table having a cup of wine.

At 4.30 pm I came to Carrion de los Condes. Normally a pilgrim coming from Fromista would stop here, because he had made his daily 20 kilometres. And besides for the next 16 kilometres there is not another village. So many of the pilgrims I have met in Fromista have stayed here. But for me 4.30pm sounded like an opportunity to walk for another couple of hours. The daylight would still be there at least until 8pm. Besides, I felt great, and the road was on the plain so there were no ascents and descents to take away extra energy. So, I decided to go on.

Those 16 kilometres are the longest distance between two neighbouring towns on the whole Camino. The road there is practically a straight line for the whole length.

Here Camino follows an old Roman road. In Roman times this used to be marshland and the Romans have built a Roman road across that swamp. And this old Roman road was actually my first experience with the spiritual part of the Camino. I remember how it came to my thoughts that two thousand years ago Julius Cesar was probably on this road with his legions (Caesar left Rome for Hispania in the spring of 49 BC to secure the province.). That thousands of Roman legionaries have marched on this road. And not just the Romans - for more than one thousand years pilgrims walk on this road. As all those thoughts crossed my mind I all of the sudden started to feel that some strong energy started to *flow* up my legs. Like it was coming from the ground up into my body. And I felt so strong. It was no problem to do those 16 km despite the fact that I had already done 20 km that day and despite the fact that it was already late afternoon as I started to walk this old Roman road.

That day I ended up with 36 km - for the first time in my life. I was amazed. I couldn not believe myself. Was all that only in my head, was all that energy that I felt on the last part of that day only a result of a strong self-motivation or was it really something beyond that? I am still trying to rationalize these things, but until now I still haven't found the clear answer. I think it will really take time. Especially because it was not the only unusual event I had on the Camino. This was only the beginning. But before my full entrance into the spiritual phase I will have to go through one more phase – the mental one. But I was not there yet.

I came to Calzadilla de la Cueza at 8.40 pm. Just at the time of the sun set. I entered a community hostel and got the last bed. I took a shower and had a small meal from my backpack. I was happy with my progress and with my physical condition. I was also happy with my equipment. The only thing I figured I didn't need any more, were my sport's shoes. For days I felt great in my trekking shoes. I decided that after ten years it is maybe really time to part from my favourite sport shoes. Farewell was a little bit emotional, since these were the shoes I had worn when I ran a 42 km marathon 10 years ago in Ljubljana, but I knew that they would be of no use any more and would be only an unnecessary burden in my backpack. They have seen enough victories. So, I let it go - I left my dear Nike Bowerman collection marathon sport shoes in Calzadilla de la Cueza.

Everybody cries on the Camino

When it happened, it was a big shock for me, since we all know that big men do not cry. But they do on the Camino. It happened to me on my third Sunday on the Camino (28.4.2019), some half an hour before I came to the midpoint of the Camino Frances.

This day started perfectly normal. Just like any other day I had a strong breakfast. There in the canteen I met Maya from Sweden. She was at the other table, and I heard that she speaks Swedish with another woman. As that woman left I wished her "Buen Camino!" and she wished me the same back. At that moment I used my small knowledge of the Swedish language and thanked her for her wish in Swedish: "Tack så mycket!" She was surprised but she left. On the other hand Maya could not resist asking me if I am from Sweden too. "No, unfortunately not, but I love your language ever since I had a chance to learn it for free for two semesters back in the nineties." That's how we started to talk. We exchanged our social media accounts, and I met her many more times later on. She was also of great help later on as I came back home and wanted to get social media contacts with the people I met on the Camino. Maya, I thank you once more, from my heart, for all of your help.

I finished my breakfast shortly after 8 am and started to walk at 8.30 am. Little past midday I stopped at Albergue Jacques de Molay in Terradillos de los Templarios for lunch. There I met Angel and Francisco, two friends of Arhuro. I have known all three of them since Logronio where we were all in the same hostel. Arturo was not with them anymore. He left for home after a week but the two of them were up to go all the way to Santiago de Compostela. We had lunch together and toasted to the rest of the Camino with large jugs of beer.

I stopped for an afternoon coffee at Restaurante Casa Barrunta in San Nicolás del Real Camino at 3 pm and an hour later I caught my first glimpse of the Sahagun. And then something unexpected happened to me.

It started as a complete surprise. I knew that I was about to come to the halfway point of the Camino. That it is over there behind the trees that I see in the distance. All of the sudden I started to feel like something was boiling up from my stomach. It was really like some bubbles in the gas water started to rise toward my head. It was pretty quick and clear to me what was going on. I knew they were the emotions. The shock was that there were so many. It was a sense of joy and pride that I have made it this far, a sense of thankfulness, that I was given the opportunity to be here and to be able to do the Camino. I was happy that I have not disappointed my family and my friends who have followed me via Instagram and Twitter.

You have to understand that when you come to the Camino you are full of doubts about your ability to finish it. I was not sure what would happen when I started my Camino. Am I going to twist my ankle? Is it going to be my knee since it always hurts when I descend? Am I going to get sick and have to stay in bed for days? Am I simply going to quit because everything will be too hard for me? I really didn't know how things would turn out. That is the main reason I didn't buy the return flight ticket. I really didn't know when I go back. It might just be only one week later after I come on the Camino. But then after two weeks of constant walking you find yourself just before the midpoint of the Camino and it becomes clear to you that despite all those doubts you made it this far. That nothing of those bads happened to you and that there is a pretty good chance that you will make it all the way to the end. You realize that your muscles have grown, that the ligaments in your ankles and knees got stronger, that your body has sweated out many accumulated poisons and that your metabolism has adapted to the new rhythm. You realize that you feel stronger and even kind of younger. And you realize that with every day that comes, the chances that something bad happens to your body, are getting smaller and smaller.

And the emotions that started to come were the consequence of all those realizations. And they started to flood me with an unbelievable force.

I did everything to fight them. I clenched my teeth, but it did little good. I also clenched my fists and started to breathe deeply through my clenched teeth. But nothing of that helped. Emotions were simply too strong. I quit fighting it and simply let it go. And it went through me like a tsunami. Tears started to flow. And I let them flow. In a minute I was completely wet. Not just of tears but also of sweat. Yes, the whole experience was so intense that I sweated like I was an athlete at the Olympics. I cried for minutes, and it felt great. It still gives me goosebumps. And I am not ashamed to admit that I cried. After all it was not the last time. The same happened to me at pilgrim mass in Santiago De Compostela. But then I haven't even tried to fight it. I simply accepted it as a part of the whole experience. Especially since by then I already knew that everybody cries on the Camino. I learned about that only after my first experience.

Twenty minutes later I come to the midpoint - at Ermita de la Virgen del Puente pilgrims come to a kind of portal in the church yard – two statues with a hint to an arch on top of them – that symbolize the geographical midpoint of the way. I was full of emotions and adrenaline. I took a couple of pictures and gave the people there my phone and asked them to take some movies of me crossing the line.

Photo session was over in minutes, and I went on but after only like 200m I had to stop. I found a shadow at the wall of the large warehouse and had to sit down. I didn't have the power to make another step. It was like a truck had hit me. A total collapse of my strength. It all came on me. I was out of the last atom of my power. And I had to rest. It is unbelievable how such an emotional storm can drain you out completely.

I sat there in the shade on a bare concrete floor, leaned back with my back to the wall of the warehouse. Other pilgrims passed by wishing me Buen Camino. I remember Jan from Sweden was one of them. I met him days ago in a little bar in the suburbs of Burgos with a furnace that stood at the wall near our table. Back then we talked about the bad weather in Montes de Oca but today I was only able to say Buen Camino back and nothing more than that. I should have said something more to Jan since we haven't seen each other for days. I should have asked him about his injured knee. I saw he was walking strangely, but I simply couldn't. It was in a total energy eclipse. Fortunately Jan 's knee got better. I learned about that when I met him 9 days later just before O'Cebreiro at the border stone marking Galicia.

Only after a quarter of an hour did I managed to take off my shoes and grab an orange juice from my backpack and drink it out. I sat there for a whole hour. Which is a lot on the Camino, since your daylight hours are limited. But I had no other choice. I need to rest. I needed to recuperate. Looking back this was just one of many totally unexpected events on my Camino.

You can prepare yourself for the Camino, you can also have some expectations, but Camino gives you so much, much more. Looking back, I can only say I am thankful for this experience of total euphoria. It is a part of the Camino experience. One of the reasons for my decision to go on the Camino was also to explore my limits. I have to admit I meant it more in a physical way. Like how many kilometres can I walk in a day, or am I able to do one hundred in three days, etc. But I have never ever imagined that I will also enter into this emotional part of the explorations. And this was just one of the early ones. Just the beginning. I believe it has shocked and shaken me so hard since it was the first one, since I was not prepared for it and since I tried to fight it. So from there on I just accepted everything that came on me.

Later that day, already in the afternoon as I entered Sahagun and went to get the certificate about passing the midpoint of the Camino I shared this experience with my followers on Twitter. As they learned about my emotions and as they saw the certificate, they got emotional too since they have also had many fears and doubts about my project. I cannot blame them since deep, deep down I know that I was the greatest doubter about it myself. I was afraid all the way that I will not finish my Camino, that something might happen to restrain me from finishing it. The only thing I never doubted was that I will do everything within my power to finish it. The rest was up on God's will. If it was not meant, so be it. I was prepared to accept that. I know it would make me sad that I did not accomplish the Camino project as planned, but I would accept it. After all, it would only mean that I will have to give it another try. I would not be the first one, nor the last one.

I met a pilgrim on the way who was trying to finish the Camino for the third time. First time it was an injury, the second time it was the disease. And even this time it looked like he would have to quit again. He lost his documents.

I was really a lucky one since everything went according to my plans already on my first Camino. And not just that, I was lucky that I got much, much more than I have ever planned or expected. So when I came to the end – to Santiago de Compostela – and visited the pilgrim mass at midday, tears came to my eyes again. This time I have not fought them. I just let them flow. I was so deeply moved by the moment that I couldn't help myself. Everything came to my mind. The whole trip, all the experiences, all the villages and towns I passed through, all the kilometres, all the days, all the struggles, all the accomplishments, all the prayers and all the people I met, all the dinners and lunches we had together and all the talks we had. A really strong emotional flood. One of the strongest moments of my Camino. I was not the only person that cried. Not just in church but also on the main square I saw many pilgrims hugging each other, eyes wet with tears of joy that they had made it. It is a truly unique experience, and it touches you deep in your heart. But that was still two weeks away.

As I finally managed to come back to myself an hour later, I entered the Sahagun. It is a nice old Meseta Town; larger than all the villages I have passed in the last two days, but still much smaller than Leon or Burgos. Since I was still low on energy my concentration was also not 100% and I got lost. I was not able to find any yellow arrows or shells to point me the way. So I asked the lady that came by about the direction. She was also a pilgrim. Her name was Helen and she was a friend of Mary.

I knew Mary. She was from the states but her mother came to the USA from Slovakia, so she told me her original name was actually Marija. Mary was on the Camino alone but she was to meet two of her friends – I think she said they would come to Leon – and walk with them to Santiago de Compostela. Helen told me about the way but she also asked me if I have got the halfway certificat. I didn't know anything about any such certificate so she told me where to get it. So I went to the museum near the pilgrims' church on the top of the hill in the south part of Sahagun.

Certificat is really nicely done. The lady in the museum writes in your name by hand and it costs practically nothing. What also counts is that the museum has air conditioning so I managed to cool myself, get another drink from my backpack and to eat the whole 100g Milka chocolate bar.

I was sitting there enjoying the chocolate as a lady and her friend came in for the certificate. After they got them, they looked around the museum but they also noticed my pilgrims shaft. So the lady approached me to ask about it. She introduced herself as Elke from Germany and I told them the story of my staff. Of Course we also took a photo together with my staff.

I left Sahagun at 8 pm. I wanted to go to Bercianos del Real Camino, but what I did not know was that I can go there directly and that there is no need to go through Calzada del Coto. Calzada del Coto is actually out of the way. No problem if you go there for their hostel, or if you are looking for some alternative way to walk the Camino, but for me definitely out of the way. So as I was at the end of Calzada del Coto I found a junction. The Camino splits there so I did not know where to go. All confused, I was looking in my phone but could not figure out where to go.

But as it always is on the Camino, help came in no time. It was an old Spanish lady from the village. She saw I was lost so she asked me in Spanish where I wanted to go. I told her I want to go to Bercianos del Real Camino. She explained to me that I have to follow the left fork of the way for about a mile and then cross the highway bridge. On the other side I will find the road that reaches my destination after two kilometres. I thanked her sincerely and wanted to go but she asked me one more question:

"Are you going all the way to Santiago de Compostela?"

"Yes, of course, that's my plan!"

"Que, por favor abrace al Santo también por mí! (Then please embrace the saint also for me)" she sincerely asked me.

I promised her I would do that, and I really did as I was there above the grave of Saint James in the Santiago de Compostela cathedral. Spanish people are very religious. And they have really a very special attitude toward the pilgrims. They saw pilgrims as a people on a mission. That is why they have a high respect for them.

And it is not just the people that you meet. It is also the people that you do business with. All the hosteleros, all the owners of the shops and all the owners of the bars, they are all very nice toward the pilgrims. Besides the religion they also know that Camino is a great part of the Spanish tourism business.

Speaking of business, I like their approach. They will never rip you with prices. Accommodation prices in hostels are very modest – something between 7 to 12 euros. And they usually include not just bed but also a pilgrim's dinner. Of Course, you can always give a higher donation. So basically, their policy is to get you to Santiago de Compostela. To feel as well as possible on that journey and to come back again and also to tell the others about the positive experience. And people do come back. I talked to people that were here for the second, third and fifth time. I even found an Australian lady on Instagram that came back for the eighth time.

So, after finding the right way to go I was in Bercianos del Real Camino with the sun set at exactly 9 pm. I was very exhausted and very happy as I met Jesus. He was the hospitaliero at the big hostel called Albergue La Perla. A very modern hostel. More like a hotel since the room that I got was a room for four persons and it had its own bathroom. I shared it with just one other pilgrim. And he was not there when I came so I quickly took a shower. Then I had to eat, and Jesus prepared me a great meal in the canteen.

I was happy to make another long-distance walk. Today it was 31 kilometres. So here on Meseta I really pushed it to my limits. 34 kilometres from Hontanas to Fromista two days ago. 36 kilometres from Fromista to Calzadilla de la Cueza yesterday and 31 today. This was 101 kilometres in total. Really a great result of extreme motivation. In those three day I have made the distance I have planned to walk for 4 days. So, I got an extra day! Finistere seemed more and more real. That night I slept like an angel. A well-deserved sleep after the emotional storm and a 100+ achievement.

Long term fatigue takes its toll

After a good breakfast I took a picture with the La Perala hosteliero Jesus and then went for shopping in the village. I was two days away from Leon. I could have split this distance in half or I could have made a longer part today and leave only a smaller one for tomorrow. As I started to walk in the morning I haven't decided yet what to do. I let it be for the moment and waited to see how it would go.

The day went on in a usual rhythm. I was on my way for more than two weeks. The pains of the first days were long gone. I managed to do more than half of my way. I yield an extra day. I was well supplied with drinks and food. I was not a rookie pilgrim any more. Yesterday's sun gave me a little sunburn on my calves but I cower-wrapped them in some scarfs, so I was OK. There were no more surprises for me on the Camino. That was at least what I had thought that morning as I walked toward El Burgo Ranero.

It was another hot sunny day so I stopped at a pharmacy in El Burgo Ranero to buy me sunblock. I got one with SPF 50 that did the job. No more sunburns like yesterday.

The Camino after El Burgo Ranero goes along a local road. The road is a straight line that follows the same direction as the railway – North West toward Leon. There are trees planted along the Camino every 4.5 meters. They were meant to give pilgrims the shadow in summer, but they are still too small to do the job. The same distance between the trees and the fact that they are all of the same size and of the same sort gives a strong contribution to the monotony of the place. The landscape is totally flat, and you still can't see the Montes de Leon. You know they should be somewhere in that same direction as you go but you still can't see them since they are hidden beyond the horizon.

So, I was walking along that local straight flat road. I was alone. And the day was hot as hell. The excitement of the first days and the excitement of the entrance to Messeta were long gone. So was the excitement of reaching the midpoint of the Camino.

All of the sudden I felt some kind of depression coming on me. I was on the Meseta for the fifth day and the landscape has not changed and there was still no sign it will. Not at least for another couple of days. I realised that Messeta is starting to take some unpredictable mental toll on me. I didn't know what to do. At 3 pm I had to stop at some little pilgrim's rest in the shadow of a road-by forest and get me some chocolate. Usually this helps as you get depressed.

I rested for like half an hour but chocolate brought no improvement. I was still pretty down and worse, I started to feel so so tired. I guess that 100+ achievement started to come after me. So it looked like some negative synergy of tiredness, temporary loss of excitement and heat of the day, descended on me like some heavy burden. Seeing trains passing by and comparing them with my speed of travel made it even worse.

I have heard that people have problems with depression on the Meseta but never imagined what this might look like. And now I was in the middle of it. Slowly this flatness bit me deeply into my very core.

Now I know that Meseta impress you with its vastness and kills you with its endlessness. It is a respectful "opponent" that you shouldn't take it easy. Meseta teaches you how small you are!

After I did all that thinking I had to go on - somehow. I guess that I hadn't drunk enough that day and was a little bit dehydrated. So, I drank all the juice I had and that helped. I made myself a mental note not to repeat this same mistake again. In the next few days an extra bottle of liquid will be in my backpack every morning. I put on some music and went on.

But the monotony of the road was still there and so was the heat and my tiredness of recent days' achievements. At 4.30 pm and only 4 kilometers later as I came to the underpass of the railroad I had to stop again. I simply collapsed down on the pavement.

I appreciate the shadow of the underpass and the fact that there it was slightly cooler than in the open. The long-term fatigue hit me with a total force. I sat there for an hour feeling pity for myself. Not something to be proud of. I exchanged some messages with my friend and adviser Nataša back at home and I agreed with her that I need to take a day of rest otherwise the circumstances might come to the point where I will not be able to finish my Camino. And that would not be just a pity but a disaster.

So, I made a plan to come to Leon and rest there. I wanted to spoil myself with some massage or maybe even go to a local swimming pool. Yes, in the shadow under the railroad I was dreaming of swimming.

As I made the decision about the day of rest, I felt much better. I had something to look forward to. Something to be excited about again. With all that in my mind I managed somehow to pull myself together and went on to Reliegos.

As you enter the Reliegos there is a shop on the left. I passed it as I didn't know it was the only one in town. Reliegos is a strange place. They have a house that looks at you. Big blue coloured house with huge eyes. Very surreal like those eyes from that big art-deco style oculist advertising board in "The great Gatsby". Only these eyes here were actually the windows of the house - very strange and very sinister.

There, in front of that house I saw "the man that had lost his passport". He was desperate since this was his third attempt to do the Camino and it looked like he would fail again. First time it was an injury, second time a disease, this time it all looked like he will have to go to Madrid to the embassy to get a new document. He appeared very lost as we spoke. The house looked at us and said nothing. Its blue colour matched with the feelings of "the man that had lost his passport".

A few streets later I met Hanne. A very nice lady from Denmark. As I asked her about the shops, she told me that she tried to find one too but there were no open shops at Reliegos. I guess in this town they were still practicing the Spanish custom of Siesta. Since there were no open shops, Hanne gave me information about the pubs and hotels. She was very nice to talk to and a great relief after the meeting with the lost man and the house from the twilight zone.

I went to the pub on the main street since it was 5.30 pm and I had to eat something. As I entered the main room of the pub it was practically empty. There was only a group of locals playing cards at one of the tables. I sat down at one of the tables and waited for somebody to come and took my order. But nobody came. Not for a minute, not for two, not for three. Only like five minutes later one of the card players rose and came to me to ask what I would like to drink. He was a bartender and also the owner of the pub. So there was no use asking for somebody that was in charge. He was in charge, but he was playing cards.

He brought me a large beer and a menu for food. Then he went back to the other card players. It lasted another hour and a couple of rounds of cards to make him come back again. I should have left with a drama but I had no energy to quarrel with him, let alone walk to the next town. So I waited and drank my beer. Game went on as those games usually do. Men shouted at each other. Cards flew on the table. There was a lot of hand movement that spoke about the card player's feelings. One of the players left prematurely. They were all totally overwhelmed with the game. Nothing else existed for them. Not either such a detail like some guest of the pub waiting to order something to eat.

As they finally stopped, the big boss of the pub finally came to me to take the order. I ordered a large steak with french fries and some wine. Luckily he was in a good mood - I guess he won at cards - so he made me a great meal. The steak was really a decent one and the portion of the fries came with a surplus. Maybe he also felt a little bit embarrassed since he forgot about me waiting there.

After I finished my meal and went to pay, he asked me if I also needed a room. I declined since this would be a little bit too much in my opinion. The meal was OK, but the attitude before that was not. So, I paid and went out. I decided not to look for another hostel in Reliegos since, to be very polite, the town was not my favourite one. I wanted to leave this "1Q84 cat town" as soon as possible.

So I left for the next town – Mansilla de las Mulas. It is like an hour away and you cross the highway again. It was late afternoon and already as I was exiting the Reliegos I started to notice that in the meantime, as I was here, the clouds gathered in the sky and it looked like thunderstorms were about to strike.

I came to Mansilla de las Mulas as the sky was just about to burst. I was not the only one in the hurry to find a decent shelter before the storm, so were the shepherds with their flocks. They stopped me for the moment as one of them crossed the main street. My friends following me back from home over my posts on Instagram commented that finally there is something to stop me. They have also felt my new energy after the decision to rest for a day in Leon.

I found a hostel just before the storm. It was a very nice modern hostel. Downstairs it was a kind of pub – half pub, half grocery store - with lots of hams, sausages and local cheeses and upstairs a large dormitory. It was only half full, so it was one of the rare occasions that I, as a latecomer, was able to choose the lover part of one of the bunks there.

After a shower I went downstairs and ordered another big meal. After all today's events I was very hungry and very thirsty. Sun, exhaustion, depression and another long daily distance took their toll and my body needed a strong refuelling - proteins, carbs and looooots of fluid.

Today we sail for Jorg!

After a good night's sleep I woke up early. The day found me in a great mood and I started it with a nice breakfast. I started to walk at 9.30 am. Tuesday's distance from Mansilla de las Mulas to Leon was a short and easy one. Just a couple of small towns, a couple of bridges and one small ascent on the hill before the capital of Castilla and Leon. All in total just 18 kilometres. I was in front of Leon's cathedral already at 3 pm.

12:45 · 30 Apr 19 · Twitter for Android

Like every other day I dedicated my walk of the day to somebody I knew. Pilgrim's walk is actually a kind of a prayer and it is a nice custom that we pray for the others. The first days of my Camino were dedicated to my family -

later on I walked for my friends. Each day in the morning I told them in my post who I walk for that day. They were all very grateful for that.

Natasa Vrtacic @nvrtacic · 01 May

Replying to @JKPsCamino

Danes pa mi hodimo za Jorga!

◯ 1   ⟳ 1   ♥ 3   ⤶

And today just shortly after I came to the cathedral my friends surprised me with a message that said: "Today we sail for Jorg!". It was a very nice gesture to say thank you for all of my walks for them. 30th of April was already the time around the May 1st public holidays and one group of my friends went sailing on the Adriatic Sea. They also sent me a great picture. I was very happy to see them and also highly appreciated that they were thinking of me as they were there. The Adriatic Sea also has a special meaning for me since my family originates from the two Adriatic islands – Korčula and Hvar.

Leon is a big city and has many hostels. But first I had to sit down and eat and drink something. I found a nice pub on the main street just meters away before it comes to the corner of the cathedral square. I got myself some tapas and a big glass of red wine. The wine tasted great, and I enjoyed the view of the cathedral and on the main street for the next hour. It felt great. An overture to tomorrow's day of rest.

I left the La Trastienda del 13 bar shortly after four to find a bed. I chose to stay at Franciscaner's hostel since they not only offered the accommodation at a great price, but also because that price also included laundry that they did for you. So I put my things in the room and gave the laundry to the hosteleros. I was happy to meet Angelo and Francisco in the room. They were not so quick after all. They were here in Leon just like me despite the fact that I was a very slow walker.

I left the hostel to spend the rest of the afternoon and the evening in the town. I wanted to find addresses of some massage salon and some public swimming pools for tomorrow. Pretty soon I have learned that tomorrow on May 1st everything is closed. So I sat at the same bar as before and enjoyed observing people passing by. I saw and greeted many of my pilgrim friends. I was most happy to learn from the "man who lost his passport" that he got it at the local police station. Somebody brought it there anticipating he might come there to ask.

At 6 pm I went to the mass in the cathedral. The service is actually not in the cathedral but in one of its chapels. After the mass I went for another glass of wine to La Trastienda del 13 bar.

Somewhere around 8 pm I felt like I needed a real meal and I decided to go to my Franziskaner hostel. The cantine there is pretty large, and it operates as a self-service. The supper there was good, but nothing special. I sat, ate and talked there with the "men who found his passport".

The day of rest in Leon

In the morning it was time to leave the hostel. Here in Leon the one-night rule was strictly enforced. So, I had to move to another hostel. One that did not ask for credentials to check the stamps. A commercial one. I found one not far away from my favourite bar. It was a Globetrotter Urban Hostel. A class one hostel with a great interior and perfect beds, showers, kitchen and especially the perfect location. Cathedral square was just like 10 meters away. And it cost just maybe 30% more than the usual hostels that I was used to going to on my Camino so far.

After accommodating I went to the Cafeteria Albany and ordered a croissant and a coffee for breakfast. As I sat there Paul came along. This time he was much better. His cold was a long-gone history. I was so happy to see he was well again. His decision was the same as mine. He was here in Leon for a day of rest. We agreed to have dinner together at 7 pm.

After breakfast I went to see some sights and ended up shortly after in my favourite La Trastienda del 13 bar again, for a midday lunch. I got another lovely message from my friends back at home. The text under the picture said: "Today we walk for Jorg." It was May 1st and it was time for their traditional hiking in to Kamniška bistrica valley. It was in the river that flows through that valley, where I picked up my stone for the Cruz de Ferro. This valley and this river are our source of life since all the water that we drink comes from that river. And the river waters come from the surrounding mountains that we all love to climb so much. So my stone was a part of those mountains and a part of that river. That had a very special meaning for me.

After lunch I played with the idea to see some sights. It would be nice to walk around Leon the whole day, but I decided to go back to the Globetrotter hostel since this was my day of rest. I slept practically the whole afternoon.

I had dinner together with Paul and Christopher. Another American, Paul, met on the Camino. We went to a great restaurant Paul recommended. The restaurant is called El Tizon.

Through this dinner I have learned what a deep person Paul is. He was really on a spiritual journey and I have learned a lot from him. Now full of energy he was a real wellspring of spiritual inspiration. Speaking to him in Leon was a great preparation for the visit of Cruz de Ferro four days later.

Christopher was a true inspiration. I liked the way he presented his ideas. Modest on the outside but a rock of religion on the inside.

The evening went by through the discussion about the religious part of our journey. We have exchanged our favorite citations from the Bible, bound to our journey here on the Camino and bound to the journey through our lives in general. We read to each other prayers from our little books of prayers and discuss the ways we practice praying along the way.

We also shared the experiences of the Camino. I remember that Paul told us how he was standing in front of some little church as a man approached him and said: "You have to enter!" It was his turning point on the Camino. He understood the call. It is not that you just walk the Camino, you have to enter its religious dimension. Everybody gets this call on the Camino - sooner or later. Even people that are not religious admit the special energy of the Camino, especially of some of its places. With his entrance into the church, Paul has crossed also the doors into the spiritual part of the Camino. Camino has transformed him in that single moment. From there on he was no longer the same person. A very strong and truly transcendental experience. A perfect example of Ultreia as my Spanish friends call it. I have learned a lot from Paul and Christopher and I highly appreciate that I was given the opportunity to meet them. This dinner talk we had, was spiritually the deepest one I have had on the whole Camino. Thank you Paul and Christopher for sharing your thoughts so frankly with me.

After Leon I haven't seen Paul for a long time. He was big and as an ex-military he must have walked greater daily distances as I did. I met him only briefly in O'Pedrouso. It was the last evening before we finished our journey in Santiago de Compostela. I was just about to go for a glass of beer with Bjorn as I saw Paul finishing his dinner in one of the restaurants. We invited him to join us but he was still firm about his alcohol fasting all the way to Santiago de

Compostela. Only there would he join us for a beer. He was truly a man of high principles and of unprecedented self discipline.

After supper we parted and everyone went to their hostel.

My recuperation in Leon showed great results

As I woke up and started to get ready for my next day walking, I saw that a neighbour in the bed just across the corridor is a pilgrim too. He was getting through his preparations too, with all the bandages and socks. His name was Robert, and he was from Spain. At that moment I didn't know that in the next few days I will be with him in a group of great Spanish and Italian friends. A group full of energy, spirit and a great sense of humour.

Breakfast, which was included in the price of Globetrotter Urban Hostel, was served in a neighbouring hotel just across the street. As I started to walk around 9 am, the streets were already pretty crowded. The walk that day was nothing special. Camino leaves Leon the usual way it leaves large towns. Through the suburbs – some residential some industrial. Officially you are still on the Meseta so the landscape was not much different as in recent days.

I stopped for the midday coffee and tortilla at Alimentación KneleB. A small little place on the left side of the road as you enter the town San Miguel del Camino. Coffee and sandwich were OK. As I went inside to pay, I noticed that they also sell souvenirs. I never paid attention to those but at that moment some wristbands caught my eye. They were made of blue silicone printed with yellow arrows, shells and some text. I took one to see what the text said, and I liked it right away. It summarises part of the Camino spirit in one single sentence: "Nunca te rindas (Never surrender)." I got one and it is still with me every day.

I came to San Martin del Camino at 5 pm. I felt great the whole day. I was full of energy and walking faster than days before was no problem. Yesterday's day of rest meant a great deal to my body. It recuperated like never before in my life! I was on the camino for 17 days before I came to Leon. And I guess by then my body and my metabolism understood pretty well how it works these days. My body understood when it's time to walk, when it's time to eat and when it is time to recuperate. My body was given those 8 night hours as I was sleeping to do all the recuperation and it did as good as it could. And then on the 18th day my body got not just 8 hours for recuperation but another extra three times eight hours in addition. And those 32 hour all together did a miracle. I felt like I could fly. I was never so fully recuperated in my life. It was a truly unique experience. I would never expect that my body in my age would still function this great. But it looks like a good daily physical activity could do miracles even as you are 50 years old.

Hostel in San Martin del Camino was half full. One room with 20 bunks was already completely full but in the second one we were only three people. This hostel was one of those where all the pilgrims sit together for dinner at the same table. The hospitaliero provided the food and we the pilgrims assisted him at cooking, preparing the table and later with cleaning. The dinner started with a prayer and as we ate I added the story of my stick as an addition to the prayer and an extra blessing to all of the pilgrims at the table.

It was a great group of people. They were predominantly young people. Only my friend Christopher and I were above 50. And yes, the hospitaliero was old too. There were actually two large groups of people at the table. One Spanish group and one Italian group and the rest of us from other parts of the world. In the first group were Anselmo, Ivan, LuiMa, Roberto, Jorge and Alba, all of them from Spain, and Marco Paulo from Italy. In the second group were Roby and Margita from Italy and Peter and Tamas, two brothers, from Hungary. The rest of us were Yola and her boyfriend, both from Spain, two Korean pilgrims and a pilgrim from Brazil. Unfortunately I do not remember their names.

During the dinner I spoke to many of them and learned a great deal about their Caminos. Ivan and LuiMa were friends from the same town. They started their Camino in Fromista and were planning to go all the way to Santiago de Compostela. Roberto and Marko Paulo both started in Leon and were also planning to go to Santiago de Compostela.

Anselmo was from Barcelona and was here just for a week so his finish was at Cruz de Ferro. He was doing the Camino in parts. This was his penultimate part and was planning to come back in September to walk the last week-part from Foncebadon to Santiago de Compostela. Later as I followed him on Instagram, I saw that he had succeeded in his plan and also that Ivan and Robert joined him and did that last part of the Camino again.

I loved it to be at such a great pilgrims dinner again. It showed how people from all over the world could cooperate, sit together, eat together, talk, laugh and enjoy simple life. We were all in such a great spirit that at the end I suggested that we all thank our host for everything that he had done for us. We gave him a great applause and he was so moved that –I will newer forget that - tears came to his eyes. That moved some of the girls at the table so deeply that they gave him a hug. It was really an evening to remember. Another beautiful experience on the Camino.

I have seen the fear of loss in women's eyes

I woke up late and most of the other pilgrims were long gone. But I was already used to that by then. I learned on the Camino that everybody has its own rhythm and its own pace. I respected that. I respect it since the Camino also in my usual life. I was a late beginner, a slow walker, but I could walk for the whole day. So usually at the end of the day we were all together again.

After I ate my breakfast, I took time to clean the table and the rest of the kitchen since I knew I was the last and did not want to leave any burden of so much work to our kind hospitaliero. I knew he had many other obligations to do – clean the bathrooms and all the rooms, change all of the beds, do the laundry, buy food and prepare everything for the new group of pilgrims. And so from day to day. I really admire all those people that take such a good care of all of us pilgrims. They are the real heroes of the Camino.

After all the work done, I thanked the hospitaliero again for his hospitality and hit the road. Being officially still on the Meseta it meant walking on the plain with no hills, valleys or other ascends and descends. And finally, I saw the mountains on the horizon. It was a sign that I will finally come to the end of the Meseta.

The most interesting place during the daily walk was Hospital de Orbigo with its famous long bridge with many arches where knights use to have duels in the Middle Ages. There is also the pilgrims hospital on the right side of the river established by the Knights Hospitaller (also known as Knights of Malta or the Order of Saint John) in the 16th century.

In the afternoon I came to my 500km point. It was on a field not far away from Astorga. Just a little bit later I come to an old stone cross on the rim of the large valley. It must stand there since eternity and many pilgrims must have come by through the times. I stopped there for a while to rest and to enjoy the great view down on Astorga.

As you come down to the valley there is a great statue of a pilgrim drinking water from its water holder. There you can also fill your bottles with water. Half an hour later, as you pass all the suburbs, you are in Astorga. At the southern entrance of the town there is a large pilgrims hostel. I checked in and took a shower, then I left to see the town. Astorga's old part is unique since it lies on a hilltop. It must have been a fortified town since the shape of the town still resembles the form of an old fortress. It has a large main square with a beautiful municipal building, many chocolate shops (Astorga is Spain's most famous chocolate town) and of course many pubs.

At one of the pubs a large group of people called my name. As I got closer, I saw that they were my friends from yesterday's pilgrims dinner. Anselmo, Ivan, Luisma, Roberto, Marko Paula, Jorge and Alba. I joined them for a beer, and we had a great time. We drank and ate there for more than an hour. We were such a nice group that the owner of the pub gave us a bottle of local wine on his account. As the sun started to near the horizon, I decided to leave them since I wanted to see the town sights, but we agreed to have dinner together at the hospital just like yesterday – all together at one table. Later at dinner I learned what a great time they have had on the main square after I left. They decided that they would have some fun and Robert announced to the people on the square that he is a famous Italian football player that is doing the pilgrimage here in Spain. All the kids there wanted his autograph on their T-shirts. And Marko Paulo suddenly went blind and started to tell stories about his one-of-a-kind pilgrimage.

Astorga has two main sights, its great cathedral and the Antoni Gaudi palace. Both are very monumental. In the church where I went to say a prayer, I met Alba. She was praying there too. As we came out, I found her very worried. I asked her what troubled her mind and she said she had prayed for her boyfriend Jorge, but did not trust me with the details. I told her I wish them all the best with whatever troubles them.

I understood her very well. I have seen that fear in the women's eyes before. I saw it in the eyes of the wives of sailors. I saw it in the eyes of the wives of alpinists. I saw it in my wife's eyes as I was leaving for Camino. It was the fear of loss. The fear of losing the men they love.

There are many stories about the Camino. But the most frightening are definitely the stories of the broken marriages. Some of them tell about them happening on the Camino, some of them tell about them happening as the people come back home.

Camino is physically and mentaly challenging and it brings you to your edges. And this is a hard test for every couple. I have heard of many couples that have quareld on the Camino. Some of them split for days, some did not meet until the end of their caminos in Santiago de Compostela. Some of them never met again.

Camino also changes the people that are there alone. Going through all the hardship and being with your own thoughts gives you a lot of time for thinking. And some people end the Camino by pooling really radical moves. One story is about a woman that was not sure about her relationship and went walking the Camino for a month - all the way to Finistere.

When a pilgrim comes to Finistere there is an old custom to burn all of your old clothes and to put on the new ones. It is a symbolic gesture of you becoming a new person. In my opinion the custom actually came from sanitary reasons. In the past the hygiene in the hostels was not as good as today (I must admit these days it is really perfect). It was quite custom to catch bed bugs. And the only way of prevention of bringing them back home, was to get rid of all the clothes one had used on the Camino. To wash and actually disinfect yourself in salty ocean water. And to put on a completely new set of clothes. These days pilgrims do almost the same. They put on the new clothes but the old ones are not burnt anymore, due to ecological reasons, but put into special containers for used clothes.

And so as that woman came to Finistere she went to the lighthouse and there she made a clear cut with all of her past. Not just that she burned all of her clothes and shoes, she also took off her wedding ring and tossed it into the ocean.

On the other hand I have seen a young couple on Instagram that have made the Camino together and as they came to Obradoiro square in front of the Santiago de Compostela cathedral, the man kneeled in front of his girlfriend, presented an engagement ring and asked her to marry him. A great ending of a great adventure and a great start of a new one.

After I left the Astorga church I went to the little square that lies just between the cathedral and Gaudy palace where local farmers had organized a cheese festival. I visited it and I must admit I haven't seen so many different types of cheese at one place in my life. It was also great to make all the degustation.

As I went back to the hostel, I stopped in a shop to buy some groceries. I brought it all to the hostel's dining room and kitchen. My friend was already there fully in action. Luisma was the master Chef and he prepared us not just a great meal but also a great cocktail afterwards. We had another great pilgrim's dinner.

To the top of the Camino

Saturday of May 4th was "officially" the last day of the Meseta. I entered it on Thursday, April 25th and now 9 days and more than 200 kilometers later I am finally reaching its end.

After I left Astorga Camino started to ascend up toward the hills at the horizon. It was a slow ascent so I did not find it too hard. I passed many villages today and stopped to find a hostel in Foncebadon.

Foncebadon is practically almost at the top of the mountain and has many hostels. I would guess there are more hostels in Foncebadon than there are inhabitants. Anyhow I picked up one of them that was not on the main street. I checked in and chose a bed. As I was pretty early, I got a lower bed of one of the bunks. In the room were already some ladies from Spain and a couple from South America. Only a day or two later I will learn that they are Giovana from Brazil and Milton from Argentina.

After a shower I went to a local Pizzeria for dinner. Pizzeria is owned by two Italians who have done the Camino and loved it so much that they decided they want to become part of it. They started their business in Foncebadon only recently. Sitting there and waiting to be served I started to talk to the gentleman sitting next to me. We spoke in English and learned only minutes later that we are both from Slovenia. What a lovely surprise. He was only the second Slovenian pilgrim that I met on the Camino.

I have learned from the two Italian owners of the pizzeria that Cruz de Ferro, which stands at the top of the mountain and is the highest point of the French Camino, is only 20 minutes' walk away. So, I decided that after dinner I will go there for a walk.

My Slovenian friend was too tired to join me so I went alone. On my way I passed another hostel and saw that my Spanish friends were sitting in front of it. They have finished their dinner as well, so I invited them to join me for the evening walk. Anselmo, Ivan, Luisma and his wife that joined him for the day from Astorga to Foncebadon and Roberto loved the idea. Jorge and Marko Paulo were unfortunately too tired so they stayed at the hostel.

We came to the Cruz de Ferro just at the time of the sunset and took some great pictures of all of us together. As it got dark most of my friends went back to Foncebadon. It was only my friend Anselmo and I who stayed a little bit longer to see how the colors of the sky would change. In those last minutes my friend from Barcelona did the best picture that I have from my Camino – the one with me ascending the pile of stones toward the pole with the cross.

So, thank you Anselmo for being such a great photographer! If this photo ever wins an award, I will share it with you 50:50. 😉👍

Back in my hostel I went to bed and wrote a short impression of the place. Cruz de Ferro is really a special place. But I will get the true impression of the place tomorrow as I will come up there with my stone.

Barrier between worlds is very thin at Cruz de Ferro

For me the experience at Cruz de Ferro was definitely Ultreia! It was way beyond anything I experienced in my life.

I left the albergue among the last. Just as usual. Milton and Giovana left at least an hour before. I went to the Cruz de Fero at 8.30 am. It was a foggy morning. It might also be that the clouds were low. Nevertheless, I was happy we took pictures of the place the evening before. This morning the photo shoot was in any way not the priority. This morning Cruz de Fero is going to be spiritual. It was about the burden and the stones. This time it was for real.

And on this misty morning the place really carried some special aura. I sensed its energy. Already back in Viloria de la Rioja, owner of the Refugio Acacio & Orietta warned everybody about that energy. It is a really unique place.

Today Cruz de Ferro was totally different from yesterday evening when I came here with my friends and the place opened to us with sky coloured in the sun set red and we did a lot of talking, photo posing and laughing. This morning I came here alone. The curtains of the morning mist were still hanging in the *air* and the place was mystically silent. As the sun was trying to come through the fog the place radiated with some special mysterious energy.

Cruz de Ferro is the highest point of the Camino but for me it was also the deepest moment of the whole Camino. From there on I entered the spiritual stage and my transformation started to happen. And it started with a bang. But let me first say something about my preparations.

I did my physical preparations, but on the Camino it was pretty soon clear to me, that there is no way you can prepare yourself for it at home. You will go through the real physical transformation only on the Camino. You will have your part of physical suffering - one way or the other - and sooner or later this physical suffering will start to challenge you mentally. You will start to question yourself why are you here suffering. And you will doubt your decision to do the Camino. That is why it is very important how well you are prepared not just physically but also mentally! I did this part of the preparations as well.

First there was a strong desire to do the Camino. As I was there, I knew it was a once in a lifetime opportunity, since when you work it is hard to get so many days of leave in a bulk. Next opportunity would probably come as I would get retired but by then I will be 15 years older and who knows if I will be able to do it.

So once I was on the Camino I was determined to do everything in my power to finish it but I was also willing to accept, if it is meant to be, that I never come to the end. I was really prepared for everything. I cleared my desk and all my drawers in the office and gave the key to my coworker. I went to say goodbye to all my friends. I even said goodbye to the people I had disputes with for years and apologized for making them angry with me. As a last step I went for a confession 2 days before I left for San Jean Pied de Port. So already before I left Slovenia I got rid of many burdens, but there was still a lot for me to carry.

As for the physical part of the preparations it is the same with your mental preparations – you can try to prepare yourself but the Camino will hit you spiritually beyond even your wildest expectations. It will go to the very bottom of your heart and soul. It will transform you and it will capture your thoughts for the rest of your days. So expect the unexpected, accept what it gives you and be open to everything. Trust me, you will come back as a different person. Spiritually and mentally transformed and your soul full of joy, peace and hope.

The iron cross - the one that gave the name to the place (Cruz de Ferro namely means iron cross) - is nothing special in itself. It is a simple iron cross on the top of a wooden pole some 8 meters high. Nobody knows who put it there.

The pole stands on a pile of stones. And this pile of stones – the very core of the Cruz de Ferro - is astonishing. I think it must be at least 4 or 5 meters high. This is kind of understandable. After all, pilgrims have been bringing the stones here for more than a thousand years - more than 10 centuries. They are coming to this place to be relieved of their burdens. Burdens that some of them are caring for decades. To put down a stone on the pile is a symbolic gesture of putting down your burden. And this gesture is more powerful than you can imagine.

Some pilgrims pick up their stones on the Camino. Some bring them from home. My stone came from the same valley as my staff. It was a stone I picked up in Kamniška bistrica river. Half of it was flintstone. Very hard and shiny white. The other half was volcanic ash - tuff. Green and very soft. So soft I was able to cut in initials with a knife. The other stone I brought there was from my mother. She is seventy five and will probably never go there. So she asked me to bring her stone here.

As you come to the Cruz de Ferro you walk a small path that goes along the road, which is on your left. Along the path, on your right, is a wooden fence. It goes all the way to the pile of stones. On the other side of the fence is a broad meadow and at its edge, just before the forest, lies a small chapel.

As I came there I first took down my backpack. I put it down on a wet grass and leaned it on the wooden fence. I unzipped the top of my backpack and took out the stones.

Then I went to the pile and climbed it. I looked around and found a spot where I was going to lay down the stones. It was not on the top but like half way up to the top, and right from the fence, some halfway toward the point facing the chapel. I got down on my knees and laid down my mother's stone first. I said a prayer for her. Then I took my stone.

At that moment I was holding my burden in my hand. It was a heavy burden I have carried for a decade. As I went for the confession before my pilgrimage I spoke about it to my priest but he said he can not help me since it has nothing to do with the sins. Nevertheless I believed I could get rid of this burden here at Cruz de Ferro. This hope kept me going and gave me strength in the hardest moments on the Camino.

I was there on my knees holding the stone with all these thoughts in my head. About all these years. About everything that I have already done with it, including the discussion at the confession. Tears came to my eyes. It was a very emotional moment. I was here and I was about to do the final act of taking this weight down from my shoulders.

And I did it. I put down my stone on the stones that were already there on the pile. Each of them with a story. All the stories different, but all full of wishes, desires, dreams and especially hopes. I put it in a small cranny between two large stones and covered it with a third one. Then I said a prayer - Our Father. Slowly and with all my heart and soul. Hand clenched together on my knees.

I was there on my knees praying and I stayed there for some time. In complete silence, contemplating the whole experience.

Then I stood up and went back to my backpack. As I got there I turned back to the Cruz de Ferro again. I looked again to the spot where I left my stone and then to the cross there on top of the pole. At that moment I decided to say another Our Father prayer. As I finished the prayer I thought to myself: »Well Jorg you have done everything that can be done to get rid of your burden. You have brought your stone all the way from home. You have walked here for more than 500 km. You went through all the sufferings of the Camino. And now you have put it down with a prayer. That's it. It is time to let go. It is time to go on.«

And then it happened. I decided to go on, so I turned to my backpack and gripped the right strap with my right hand. I swung it to my shoulders and at that moment I got completely sprayed with water. All over my face and head and shoulders. I was completely wet. I was shocked. I did not know what happened.

But after a while it all came clear to me. I always carried a bottle of water in a belly strap pocket of my backpack. And at this very moment it opened up and the water from it sprayed me. It has never opened before and it has never opened afterwards. But at precisely this moment the cork went off.

I understand the whole physics of the event - impulse equals the change in momentum. Cork was no doubt purely attached. And the impulse given to the water in the bottle, by the swing of the backpack to my shoulder, popped the cork off and let the water out and all over me. But this is only the physical part of the event. For me it is the other part that is more important. Because for me it was a clear message that I got a blessing from above that I have got rid of my burden. And this part was really wonderful. I didn't mind being all wet. On the contrary. I was totally happy. Overwhelmed with joy and thankfulness. I stood there and started to laugh and then the tears came again. It was unbelievable.

You can tell me that it was a coincidence, a random event. I have no problem with that. But it is a really rare event. I mean this bottle could have had opened many times. You have to understand that by then I was on my way for three weeks. But it had never opened before. It opened at that very moment as I finished putting down my burden. I do not mind what you think. For me the message was totally clear: »Jorg you have been released of your burden with a blessing.«

The rest of the day was a descent toward the Molinaseca and later on a short walk to the town of Ponferada.

The descent was hard since it is a steep one and I made many breaks since my left knee hurt. All the villages along the way down to Molinaseca are some of the nicest villages on the whole Camino. Many houses have been renovated and I like the way they have done it in a traditional local style – in stones and wood.

Molinaseca is some kind of a tourist resort. A very nice place. One can tell there has been a lot of money invested in a tourism business. It is another Camino place that stands at an old Roman bridge. I stopped there and an American lady took a great picture of me with the bridge and the local church. This photo is one of my favorites from the Camino. It kind of holds the energy I brought down from the Cruz de Ferro.

Ponferrada is an old town with Templars fortress that lies on a rock above the confluence of two rivers. It must have been a very strategic place in the past since the fortress is huge and must have been accommodating a large army of knights templar.

In Ponferrada I found myself a hotel. Yes a hotel, not a hostel. I wanted a room with a bath since my knee and my leg muscles hurt from the descent. The bathtub did a great job. In less than an hour I was like new and able to do the sightseeing of the town. But I had to eat first.

Since Ponferrada is a pretty large town I was also able to find a McDonald and get myself a large hamburger. I kind of felt like I needed a large portion of meat for my muscles. After I finished my Big Mac I went to walk around the town. It was already night but Spanish towns are not sleepy ones. Not even on Sunday evening. So all the pubs were open and full of guests. I looked around to find any of my friends but had no luck. So I went back to my hotel to get some good sleep.

I meet Giovana, she is a famous Brazilian actress

I left my hotel in Ponferada at 10 am. I had a long sleep in my hotel bed and a slow breakfast in the hotel restaurant.

It was Monday morning so the streets were pretty crowded. I first stopped at a roundabout where I knew there was another web camera on the Camino and took some camera webpage screenshots with me at the roundabout. Next I had to stop at some grocery store for my daily stock of orange juice, some little snacks and a couple of cans of beer – just in case I meet my friend and we decide to have an evening party.

In the shop I met Milton so after the shopping we walked together. Giovana was nowhere to see so I asked him about her. He explained that he went shopping and she went to walk the original way around Ponferada. But they will meet where the main road and the Camino join at the outskirts of Camponaraya.

And so it was. We met her and stopped in the first pub for a coffee. Milton introduced Giovana as a famous Brazilian actor but she was too modest to brag about that. She came on the Camino in a Holy week and did some early parts of the Camino by bike.

Milton joined her later. He was from Argentina. He was a big, well trained sportsman. A mountain climbing and windsurfing instructor - it dependant on the location of his work. He has spent some of his summers in the USA at the beach and some back at his Patagonia mountains. I learned a great deal about them both. The only thing I wasn't able to figure out was, if they were a couple or just friends. But this was anyway none of my business.

Both of them were very nice people and I really enjoyed the talk we had there, drinking coffee in the garden of Cafeteria Meson el Reloj en Camponaraya.

We parted with a traditional Buen Camino and I walked alone for the rest of the day. I passed Cacobelo – a very nice town in the middle of a wine country – at 2.30 pm and came to Vilafranca at 4 pm. By then I was already pretty hungry so I had to stop for a meal. I found a nice restaurant with the tables in front of it and ordered paella, beer and a coffee. I sat there as Giovana and Milton came by. They said they would join me, but went to put their things in the hostel first.

As I waited for them another couple showed up. It was my dear Hanne from Denmark, that I first met in Reliegos, and her husband. They sat down next to me and ordered something to eat and I told them the story of my pilgrim's staff.

As Giovana and Milton came we made a photo together with my famous staff. I left them shortly after. It was already past

6 pm and I had a plan to do some more walking until the end of the daylight.

I have walked all the way to Vega de Valcarce. As I came there it just started to get dark, so I decided to stop walking and to find a bed in the local hostel. Municipal hostel in Vega is not on the main street. It lies at the edge of the village up on the slopes of the valley. As I came there I was not sure where the entrance was so I asked the gentleman on the balcony where to enter. He showed me the stairs and told me to come up. There it turned out it was not a balcony but the upper terrace of the hostel that was also a hostel's kitchen. There sat two gentlemen. The one that invited me up introduced himself as Bjorn from Sweden and the other as Edwin from the USA. They offered me wine, bread and ham. I asked about the registration and Bjorn told me that for that we had to go downstairs. So we went and he registered me for one night. Now I was not sure about him. Was he really Bjorn or was he a local that joked with me that he was from Sweden. Only later during the evening he disclosed that the joke was about the registration. We laughed a lot about his joke. As we sat there and drank, Bjorn and Edwin were doing some cooking and they invited me to join them for supper. It turned out that the three of us were practically the only guests in the hostel. There was also a girl from Japan. Her name was Juko, but she went to sleep shortly after I came to the hostel. Bjorn told me that the hosteliero had left the facility more than two hours ago since no one expected that on Monday evening at something like 8 pm another pilgrim would show up at the hostel doors. But here I was.

I excused myself for a brief shower and as I came back I brought some cans of beer from my backpack. We ate dinner and talked and talked and talked. Bjorn was an architect and Edvin was in financial business. As we finished all the food and our glasses went dry we had to do something so we could talk some more. So we decided to go to the local pub. There we had some more beer and a lot more talking. It was one of the most talkative evenings I had on the Camino. We went to bed past midnight.

As I woke up Bjorn and Edwin were already leaving. Juko was already gone. I packed my things as well and went downstairs to find the hosteliero. Yesterday I was too late to meet him but today it looked like I was too early. Nobody was there at the reception. So I just left the money and my passport data at the hostelieros table. It was no problem since I was the last guest leaving.

On the street I went to the first grocery and as I came out I met Mary from the USA. She was now already with her two friends. They joined her as planned in Leon to walk together all the way to Santiago de Compostela. And as I talked to her Hanne and her husband came along too. Of Course we all took a great selfie.

Ascend to O'Cebreiro was not an easy one especially after a late night drinking, but on the other hand it was also not a hard one. I made only one stop. It was in La Faba where I had a small meal.

O'Cebreiro is already in Galicia. And Galicia is the final region of the pilgrimage to Santiago de Compostela. The border stone stands some two to three hundred meters before O'Cebreiro. It is a large one, decorated with Galicia's coat of arms. There I met Jan from Sweden whom I last saw in Sahagun. Back then his leg hurt, but now he was already perfectly OK.

We walked together toward the top of the hill and came to O'Cebreiro at 4pm. There, on O'Cebreiro, Jan helped me take the pictures in front of the church. The church on O'Cebreiro is the oldest church on the Camino since it was built in the ninth century. I visited it to say a prayer and to light a candle for my ancestors. Jan did the same.

Later, as we came out of the church I met my friends from San Martin de Camino hostel. Roby and Margita, two girls from Italy, and Peter and Thomas, brothers from Hungary. It was nice to see them again. They were now a kind of group on their own. They told me they will spend the night here on O'Cebreiro and I told them that I will walk further for another couple of hours.

Before I left O'Cebreiro I sat down in one of the pubs and had something to eat. I used the opportunity to put on my warm underwear and all of my rain gear since it started to rain.

O'Cebreitos hotel is at the end of the village. It is one of the most beautiful hotels on the Camino with a perfect view down on the Galician valleys. It also has a webcam so I took another opportunity to take some good screenshots of me on the Camino webcams.

From O'Cebreiro on the Camino goes along the local road.
On the pass of Saint Roque the weather already perfectly
matched the statue there. The wind blow like hell. And
shortly after it also started to rain again. My rain gear

protected me well but I had to find a shelter. My plan was to walk all the way to Triacastela, but yesterday's partying took a toll so I had to stop at Fonfria. The hostel in Fonfria is a big one. With a large dormitory and a big living room. It also offers a pilgrims dinner in a big house just across the street. The dinner house is special because it is made in a local architectural style. It resembles a great tent.

I came to dinner among the last and was happy to see that Bjorn and Edwin were already at the table. So we all did the same distance today. There at the table I met also Nikolas from Bruxelles, Phillip from Padova, Italy, who told me that he has a traveling agency in Ljubljana, Slovenia, and two sisters Stefany and Jessica. Jessica had a strong cold. She coughed constantly. She was the younger sister. And she was really young - practically still a child. I remember me wondering how can such a young girl be here on the Camino without her parents. I would never let my daughters do the Camino alone. Not at least as long as they are still minors. But I guess her sister was old enough, for their parents to trust her, to take good care of her. I also met Alessia and Massimo from Italy.

The dinner was a loud one since they let the music play and Spanish pilgrims started to dance - some of them also on the tables. It was a great party. After the dinner was over, we all came back to the hostel and I sat down with Bjorn and Edwin for a glass of scotch. Today we were not so talkative. I guess we were a little bit tired from last night. But being tired was OK since that night, despite the large number of people in the room, I had no problem sleeping.

Coming to Saria means you are just 114 kms from SdC

The 25th day started with a hard descent toward Triacastela. It was windy but fortunately there was no rain. Descent was a real challenge for my knee, but I managed it with the help of my walking poles. They helped me transfer much of my weight from my left leg to my arms.

In Tricastel I was finally down in the valley. I stopped in Tricastela for a meal and to do some thinking. This was the last steep descent before Santiago de Compostela. In the next few days the Camino would go through Galician countryside where the hills are no more than 100 meters high. And yes today I was also just 4 to 5 days away from Santiago de Compostela. I couldn't believe that I made it already that far. It was also here in Tricastele where it came to me for the first time, that it will all be over very soon. I will reach Santiago de Compostela and I will have to return home to my normal daily life.

While eating my meal and doing all that thinking somewhere at the back of my brains another set of calculations started. Calculations about the possibility of going further than Santiago de Compostela – to go all the way to Finistere. Here in Triacastela it all of the sudden seemed to be doable with just a little bit of extra effort. If I could make it to Saria today I would be far ahead of my schedule, despite my day of rest in Leon. That thought felt great and it gave me an extra push.

Leaving Tricastela I met Juko from Japan again. We met at the point where Camino splits in two ways. One way goes over the hills and the other, a little bit longer, goes through valleys and it also passes the famous Monastery in Samos.

I did not want to do any more ascents or descents today, so I chose the way over Samos. Juko did the same. I lost her shortly after, because I hurried up a little bit, since it was almost midday, and I knew I still had 24 kilometers to go.

Samos Monastery is worth seeing. Not just seeing but also staying there overnight. It offers good accommodation to the pilgrims, and they can also go on a tour through the monastery. I would like to stay there but I had to sacrifice that wish for my Finistere goal.

In Samos I was already pretty tired so I stopped for lunch. I sat there and ate slowly struggling to find strength to go on. Only at 4 pm I was able to go on. There were still 14 kilometers in front of me. The weather was still very windy and the clouds flew over the sky. Now and then they would bring a quick shower and just minutes later the sun would make it so hot that you had to take off all of your rain gear, the one that you just put on minutes before - a pretty exhausting exercise. I remember it was hard to find motivation and strength but I kept on pushing. It is interesting how the mood can change in just a couple of hours. That afternoon was one of those when you have enough of everything. When all of the sudden all you want is everything to be finally over. I guess my bad mood came due to the tiredness of the morning descent – it was really hard – and due to the bad weather.

Just a little before Saria I saw the first Eucalyptus tree. Now I knew I was really in Galicia and not far away from Santiago de Compostela. I had remembered that when I was here in the nineties, driving around Spain and Portugal with my girlfriend (now my wife) that I found it interesting what a large eucalypt forests are growing in this part of Spain. I guess it must be the climate that they favour – a kind of ocean influence with mild winters and enough rain in summer. Anyhow, here in front of Saria it was still just one tree – far from a big eucalypt forest – but a first sign of where I was coming.

I came to Saria at 7.30 pm. Finally! I made 31 kilometres that day. When I think it back now, I know I should have taken that other way, the one over the hills since it is 9 kilometres shorter. It is worth going to Samos, but only if you intend to stay there.

In Saria I stayed on the main street. I found a great hostal there. It is called Andaina. It was full of pilgrims that were just about to start their pilgrimage. Saria is namely the ultimate starting point since from there it is just a little bit more than 100 kilometres to Santiago de Compostela and if you want to get your Compostela certificate you have to walk more than 100 kilometres. Saria is also a great starting point because you can come there by train.

After accommodating I asked the hosteliero to advise me on the local pubs where I would get a good supper. Luckily one good restaurant was not far away. It was Hotel and restaurant Roma. The restaurant is in the basement, but it was the most classy restaurant I visited on my whole Camino. And on top of the visual experience, they offered a great pilgrims dinner for a great price. I was more than satisfied and I gave the waiter a good tipp.

Somebody walked behind me

Camino leaves Sarria over another Roman bridge. This one is small but like all the others well maintained. I remember thinking about what durable constructions those Roman bridges are. They were built 2000 years ago, and they still serve their purpose. Astonishing.

My goal that day was to walk to Portomarin which is a usual destination for all the pilgrims that start their Camino in Sarria. And I saw many. It was a big difference how many people were here on the road compared to the parts of the Camino where I walked for hours without meeting anybody. Some of those rookie pilgrims were organised in groups. And I was surprised as I saw one of those groups to be met with a van bringing sandwiches and tea for their stop. Of course, none of them had been carrying a backpack. I guess the other van must have been taking care of their language. But as I already said once: On the Camino you stop judging people. Everybody has its own pace and its own way of walking through his or her life. But I still found it "interesting". OK, to be honest I judged them. I know I shouldn't have, but after all, I too am only human and that group was really an extreme exception.

That day was also special because the Camino brings you to a point of 100 kilometres distance from Santiago de Compostela. Here in Galicia the way is well marked with the milestones on practically every couple of hundred meters so you can constantly follow your progress. And somewhere in the middle between Sarria and Portomarin stands a stone with a 100 km mark. I guess this stone is the most photographed stone in the Camino. Everybody stops there to take a picture with it. So did I.

Weather throughout the day was bad. It started to rain somewhere around midday, and it rained the rest of the day. But it was no problem since my rain gear kept me dry.

So I walked there in the late afternoon. I must have been somewhere between As Rozas and Moimentos or between Moimentos and Marcadoiro. The rain was pouring and I had just a couple of kilometers to Portomarin. Camino there is just a narrow gravel covered path. It goes through the forests and over the fields. And in one part in the middle of those fields something strange happened to me.

I was there with my own thoughts walking. I have been thinking about the novel I read years ago – Pillars of the Earth by Ken Follett - where medieval girl Aliena of Shiring in love with a boy named Jack Jackson, walks the Camino to find him. They lived in the 12th century. That brought me again to the thinking on how many people have walked this path through the centuries. What were their destinies? Where on different graveyards from England to Italy do they rest?

And then it happened.

It was past 5 pm. I was walking. The rain was pouring. All of the sudden, walking that gravel path I heard steps of someone approaching me from behind. I did the usual. I step aside to let that other pilgrim pass me. It was a narrow path after all and I was walking slowly. I waited for a moment but he hadn't passed me, so I turned around to see what stops him. But as I turned back, nobody was there!

I did hear the steps, for this I was sure. I was shocked. It was spooky. I didn't know what to do so I crossed myself and said a prayer. It looks like my thoughts have attracted some lost soul, still wandering the Camino, trying to find its peace. Such a Shiryo definitely needs lots of prayers.

Speaking of contacts with the souls from the other side it reminded me of the event we had in our family years ago. We call the story "Sava river" and it goes like that.

Sava river

"I would like to have the Sava river on my cake!" says five-year-old daughter thoughtfully.

After these words, the conversation in the car stops. The car radio was never turned on this ride so there is complete silence in the car. It is that moment of silence that the Japanese call "ma". The so-called time void or negative time. Time for reflection.

All the other passengers in the car are pondering their heads how do you put the Sava river on a child's cake and where for the God sake did the child get such a crazy idea in the first place.

It is quarter to six in the afternoon and my wife and my three daughters are on their way to the Patisserie in Kamnik, to order a birthday cake. Tomorrow is the 4th of July 2008 and my youngest daughter will be two years old.

The silence is broken by eight-year old daughter, that says: "I would like to have a Barbie ballerina on the cake." Shortly before that, they have picked her up after her ballet training. During the conversation, my wife manages to ask our daughter why the Sava river, but after her short answer that she doesn't know, she doesn't ask any further. The conversation that follows is as usual as always. The cake ordered for tomorrows party will be decorated with Pooh bear, my youngest daughter favourite fairy tale character.

The memory of this strange wish would easily have sunk into oblivion, like another of the strange children's babbling, if I hadn't sat down in front of the television with my wife in a good hour later to watch the evening news. It begins with terrible news.

"Today at 5:30 p.m., a tragedy occurred on the Sava near the Blanca Hydroelectric Power Station. Two boats overturned while crossing the spillway of the dam. 11 people are missing. Three women were rescued from the water. One died on the way to the Brežice hospital. The other is fighting for her life in the Novo mesto hospital. Eyewitnesses are reporting that when the two canoes sailed across the overflow section of the dam, they first heard shouts of excitement, which in the next moment turned into screams of terror."

At this moment, my wife turns off the television. I look at her in astonishment, and when I almost start to protest, she describes the incident that took place in the car at the time of the accident. The woman is pale, and her voice is shaky. The hair on my back and on my head stands. I do not know what to say. My mind wanders everywhere. That night, neither of us closes the eyes.

Children's souls are young. They still have a vivid memory and a strong bond with the astral world. It can also be called the world of angels. Some of them are still one with God. We can say that they are still enlightened.

However, living in the transition between two worlds is not easy. Liminal phases are always extremely stressful. Accepting and learning everything that is from this world and at the same time receiving all the vibrations or messages from the other world is too much for the small people. If a child wants to survive, he must find a balance in this world, so his brain starts to switch of certain connections. Some chapter need to be closed.

It is the ego that draws the veil of Parokhet. This is the solution at that moment. The child finally enters our world. His thoughts are freed from the unbearable noise of the liminal phase. The soul is finally embodied/incarnated.

On Camino barrier between worlds becomes permeable

Later on as I come back home I have followed Instagram posts of pastor Brian Zahnd walking the Camino. He gave a great definition of the phenomenon. He wrote that here on the Camino, because of its unique character and its energy, the barrier between both worlds practically vanishes. It becomes just a thin membrane and both worlds start to interfere.

These are his exact words: "It is a 500-mile path that has been made sacred by the millions of pilgrims who in faith have trod trillions of steps over the past thousand years, thus making it a "thin place" – a place where the barrier between heaven and earth has been worn thin and becomes quite permeable. All who walk the Camino eventually become aware of this – even those who began walking as convinced secularists. The Camino de Santiago is a testament in a secular age to the truth that there are sacred places in this world!"

Later I did a lot of thinking about that and I tried to rationalize it somehow. It would be perfectly normal that in the afternoon, as you have walked for more than 10 hours during the day and as you have already passed more than 30 kilometres, you would feel a lot of pain in your muscles. But after so many days you do not feel it anymore. After more than three weeks of constant walking the body reaches some special status. Its metabolism and all the chemical processes adapt to the struggle. Human body fights the pain with the production of endorphins. They are painkillers and they have the same side effects like the ones we take as medicine. They are not just killing the pain; they are also lifting up our spirit. Many long distance runners know that effect of a kind of being high on its own body chemistry. In such a status, the mind loosens its control and subconscious gets the chance to penetrate it.

In many religions people try to reach that special state of mind to come closer to the divine; to become more open to the spirits from the other side. That state of mind is called trans. In some religions it takes days if not years of meditation to get there. In some religions they use chemicals from different sorts of plants to make a shortcut. Some religions are using constant monotonous movement. The most famous are Rumi's sufi Dervishes that spin around for hours.

I think that constant walking has the same effect. It brings you to a kind of trans. It is to be mentioned that the experience I had first happened only after many days of walking and usually in the afternoon after many hours of daily walking.

I discussed it with the world class expert on kinesiology and its psychology; and he 100% confirmed my convictions (FlowCode – Project Unity: https://youtu.be/9aLohQAoVR8).

Anyhow, I understand the chemistry of our bodies, but I also believe in God. On the Camino pilgrims come close to that spiritual or divine world. I knew I had entered that phase of the Camino myself back with my experience at the Cruz de Ferro, but I was never expecting to encounter any more of such experience. But this here was just the next step.

I came to the Portomarin bridge an hour later. There I met Stefany and Jesica, the two sisters I met at the dinner at Fonfria. Jessica was much better. Her cough was over. It looks like Stefany really took good care of her. As I took time to take some pictures with the bridge they were long gone.

On the other side of the bridge I came to the famous Portomarin stairway to heaven. I climbed to the top but I did not pass the city gates. My plan had changed. Despite all the rain it was still some daylight to be used for some more walking. So I went on.

I came all the way to Gonzar and found a bed at Casa Garcia. I was too late for dinner. The kitchen has been already closed but seniora managed to find me a bowl of soup and a piece of delicious cake, so I was fine.

After the dinner I went to the dormitory where everybody was already asleep. I took a shower and picked up some pieces of my clothes that needed to be dried. I took them to the living room and hanged them above the radiator. I put my shoes there as well. Not that any of them were wet of rain. They were only pretty moist of sweat. The whole day of walking left its mark.

Octopus in Melide

The rain stopped overnight and I woke up in a sunny morning. I noticed that Alessia and Massimo from Italy were in the same room. I said good morning to both of them and started to pack quickly. I was full of energy and eager to do as many kilometres today as possible.

I hit the road at 9 am and kilometres went by more quickly than any day before. I was now fully in Galicia and eucalyptus forests were all around. I reached the 80 kilometres stone at 10 am and the 69 kilometres stone at 1.20 pm. I came to Palas de Rei shortly after. There I met Edvin and we decided to have lunch together. He stayed in Palas de Rei but I went on.

At 5 pm I marked the 700 kilometres point at the bridge in Ponte Campana and two and a half hours later –at 7.30pm – I was in Melide. At that time my friends Giovana and Milton were in Portomarin.

Alessia and Massimo were there too so we agreed to go for dinner together. Since we were in Melide, we went for their famous octopus. As we just sat down another familiar face came by. It was my dear friend Bjorn from Sweden.

We sat there and enjoyed the delicious octopus and beer. Alessia and Massimo were friends from the same town in northern Italy. They went here together to have a good time. They did not speak much English so I tried some of my Italian. It was as bad as their English so we laughed a lot. Luckily there was uncle's Google translator to help us.

Bjorn was a great person to talk to at dinner. And not just for dinner, but also during the day while walking. I knew that now for days. I had a great friendship with him. Of course. If you know someone on Camino for four day it means that you are already old buddies. The two friends from Italy were also great people (all Italians are) and I really enjoyed their company. We had a great time at that octopus diner in Melide.

Were those gitanes real?

Saturday 11th of May 2019 was another quick walking day. I was only a day away from Santiago de Compostela and bursting with energy. In that part of Galicia Camino goes through a flat countryside so it was no problem to do another long distance. And by now my body was already a perfect walking machine.

I do not remember many details of the day. I only remember a pink Seat 600 that I found very interesting since in our country we had the cars of the same shape, though there they were Zastavas and in neighbouring Italy they were Fiats.

During the day I stopped once to have a snack. And just as I finished my paella, Alessia and Massimo came by so I had an extra ice cream with them. We then walked together for a while and then I lost them.

I found Alessia and Massimo again at Ribadiso bridge. I just went to a nearby house to ask one of the three girls sitting there at the water to take a picture of me on the bridge. As the picture was taken I thanked the girl for taking it and also sent my hello to the two friends of hers. Filomena, who took the picture, corrected me. The other two girls were not her friends but her daughters. I made a mistake, but it actually made her proud. Just as I said goodbye, Alessia and Massimo came over the bridge so we walked together again.

I also remember passing an interesting pub with a garden decorated with many empty bottles of Peregrina beer. Bottles had inscriptions from people who emptied them so it was interesting to see from how many countries people came by.

And as I was just to come to my daily destination O'Pedrouso I experienced another interesting encounter. It was in Santa Irene. I came to a resting place for the pilgrims – a small park. There at the entrance I saw a board. A board that was there to inform about the name of the park. I only saw it with the corner of my eye since I was walking pretty quickly and I noticed it at the last moment, just as I passed it. It said that the name of the park was something with gitanes.

The word gitanes caught my thoughts and I remembered that in French it means gypsies. And at that very moment as this thought flashed through my thoughts, I saw two gypsies sitting on the grass in the park. I was walking and looking at them but they did not notice me. For me it was like watching a scene from a movie. It was a young couple. A man and a woman. She has been laughing and telling something to him. He smiled back. I passed them in seconds wondering how come they were so preoccupied with each other not to notice me. And at that moment as I was thinking about them I noticed another gipsy. It was an old man, standing on the grass near the exit of the park. I looked at him and he was looking directly into my eyes. As I approached he was still looking into my eyes. I said "Buenas tardes" a greeting used in Spain in the late afternoon but he said nothing. He stood there totally motionless, just staring deeply into my eyes. And through the whole time of our eye contact, he never blinked with his eyes. I passed him and at that moment I was not sure if all what just happened was real. Was it really possible that at the very moment as I comprehend the meaning of the word on the board they materialised there. Were those people real or were they just the product of my imagination? I wasn't even sure if the board was really there.

But I was so shaken by the event that I did not dare to look back and check if the old man I saw was still there. I was afraid that I might, just like back then when I heard the steps, turned around and found nobody. It was a late afternoon again. The watch was showing 7 pm.

At the outskirts of O'Pedrouzo the mile stone distance already dropped under 20. Tomorrow I will be in Santiago de Compostela in no time. I entered the village and found a nice hostel. There in front of my hostal I met my dear friend Bjorn and just as we discussed about a beer and a dinner Paul came by. So we invited him for beer as well. But he was still fasting, so we respected his decision to decline it. I went inside to check in, drop my backpack and take a quick shower. In less than half an hour I was already sitting on the main street with Bjorn drinking beer. Afterwards we went for dinner together.

For me it was octopus again and he took a steak. We agreed that tomorrow we would walk and enter Santiago de Compostela together. But we would have to start early if we are to catch the midday mass for pilgrims. So we set to meet at 6 in front of the hostel.

Santiago de Compostela

As planned, Bjorn and I met in front of the hostel at 6 a.m. and started to walk our etapa from O'Pedrouzo to Santiago de Compostela. It was still pitch dark so I put on my head light. As we came to the Amenal we decided to stop for breakfast. We found an inn just as we came through the passage under the road. It was a self-service restaurant except for coffee. Coffee was to be ordered at the bar and it took an eternity to get one. But we waited patiently because there was no other option. After finishing our croissants, orange juice and coffee we went on. We exited the inn just as dawn started and within minutes we had daylight to do the walking.

Next couple of hundred meters the Camino goes through a trench. A deep trench. I have seen many parts like that on the way and it always fascinated me how deep into the ground the Camino came. I always thought of billions and billions of steps made by pilgrims through the centuries. And those steps had that effect. They have rubbed the path deep into the ground. In many places the steps have carved the Camino all the way to the bedrock. And not just that at some parts even that bedrock has been grinded feets deep. But nowhere through the whole way it looked like this trench here. Maybe even the word trench is not a sufficient expression to describe it. Maybe I should say gorge.

And that gorge looked very mystical as we were passing through it. The morning light just started to show and the morning fog still hanged around. The colours were still a little bit darkened. Especially all the green tones of the moss, that grew on the tree trunks and on the rocks and stones of the gorge walls. I think we passed it in a perfect moment. It added one last great impression of all of the places on the Camino that the passing souls have cut deep into the ground. My thoughts at exiting it were that every step that made that carving have added just a tiny little cut. With the energy of each step a tiny piece of dust has been chipped away from the rock. Maybe just a few layers of atoms were taken away. Practically nothing. But through the time it has had such a profound effect. I remember some parts of the Camino where the path looked like a river bed full of round stones. And now it came to me that those stones were not shaped by water, but by the flow of the river of pilgrims, walking to Santiago de Compostela through the centuries.

And it was not just the steps that left the physical mark on the Camino. All of those positive people, full of good will, full of prayers, full of will to help each other, all of those pilgrims have also left that kind of positive energy on the Camino. It was to be sensed all around. It was just a question of time when you become sensitive enough to feel it. For me it was already days back, as I was on the old Roman road between Carrion de los Condes and Calzadilla de la Cueza. But here it was much, much stronger. No wonder. I was just kilometres from Santiago de Compostela, where that river of positive energy has been flowing to. And as it tends to be, the river grows on its way and reaches its peak **Flow** just at the spot where it enters the ocean. The same was with the Camino. No doubt, the energy of the Camino there in the gorge has been very strong. After all, we were almost at Santiago de Compostela.

An hour later we were at the airport fence. Yes, the Camino pases along another airport (first one being before Burgos). Nothing special there. Just a hint that you will be flying home soon.

At Lavacolla we stopped to do the traditional pilgrim's ritual of washing. It is known that through the centuries pilgrims have stopped in Lavacolla to make the laundry. It was a question of respect toward the saint. One can not enter the cathedral all dirty and smelly from the road. Back then there was not like today, where you can find a washing and a tumble drying machine in every hostel. Lavar means to wash in Spanish and there is actually really a little stream that flows through the village of Lavacolla. Well we haven't actually washed our clothes but we washed our hands and faces. It was our humble gesture to show we pay a tribute to the Camino traditions.

Santiago de Compostela is practically just a hill away from Lavacola. Once you come on top of that hill you can already see the city. That is why the hill is called Monte Gozo – the hill of joy. We came there after a brief stop in Vilamajor for a cup of coffee and one last stamp in our pilgrims credentials.

The time of arrival on Monte Gozo was 10am. City of Santiago de Compostela lay in the valley in front of us and it looked magnificent in the morning sun. No wonder it is traditional for the pilgrims here, as they saw the towers of the Santiago de Compostela Cathedral for the first time, to kneel down and thank God for the safe journey. And that was exactly what Bjorn and I did.

But first we had to put on clean clothes. I changed into a fresh cotton shirt and fresh cotton pants from my backpack. Now I was ready to enter the city, I was ready to enter the main square and I was ready to enter the cathedral. But first I was ready to kneel.

So I kneeled down on Monte Gozo in front of Santiago de Compostela and said a prayer of thanking. Deeply from my heart I thanked God to lead me safely here toward my pilgrimage destination.

Then it was down the hill and across the highway bridge. At the roundabout we came to the famous Santiago de Compostela sign, written in large red letters full of stickers. It was 11am and we still had to walk across the whole town to get to the cathedral. It was still our plan to attend the midday pilgrims mass. Walking through the town we learned from other pilgrims that the pilgrims masses are currently held at San Francisco church since the cathedral is under renovation.

It was Sunday, the God's day, and the town was fully in that spirit. People on the streets have been singing hallelujah. The whole atmosphere was unbelievable. The river of pilgrims has been mowing toward the main square. We knew we were almost there as we heard the sound of pipes. At that very moment you are just down the stairs, through the arch and on the left. And you will be there - at the end of your journey.

The two of us entered the Praza do Obradoiro in front of the Santiago de Compostela cathedral at 11.45, the sound of pipes still in our ears. I cannot express my feelings at that moment. I lack the words of high enough magnitude to describe them. It felt magnificent. After crossing 765 kilometers, after walking for 27 days and having only one day of rest I was finally here on the very end of my pilgrimage.

My friend Miha, the one that made my pilgrim's stick, commented that this was a moment of the triumph of will and the victory of the faith. A comment meant in the pure meaning of the words.

I stopped there at the centre of the square and raised my pilgrims pole high above my head. I was full of energy. I was full of pride. I made it. I was the winner! That moment was unforgettable. It will stay in my memory for the rest of my days! I was finally at the very point where all the caminos meet. At the point where all the rivers of energy come to their end and transfer their energy to the place. No wonder it bears the name of the field of stars. It is a proper name for the focal point of Camino energy. Energy of millions of stars – energy of millions of pilgrims that came here through more than one thousand years.

And like all the centres of fire it emits that energy all around it. Every person that comes to the square, being a pilgrim or just a visitor, takes a little bit of that positive atmosphere from the square with him back home. Even people that are not religious can't deny the positive influence of the atmosphere there. Just seeing the happy people coming to the square after many hard days of walking, warms the hearts of the people on the square. If you manage to think about their stories, about their aspirations, burdens that they have carried, friends that they have met, and all the rest of the different Camino facets, it definitely touches you deeply into the very core of yours.

The Camino focal point is like a polished diamond. The light comes in to its center from all the directions but then it emits it back out, transformed into the beautiful colours of the rainbow. This energy, taken by the people back home to all different parts of the world, brings them back on the Camino. And not just them, but many, many others.

So as I stood there with my stick above my head, enjoying the energy burst, Bjorn took a picture of me. It is definitely one of the most energy full pictures of me that I have. Bjorn felt the same. He was happy and proud. Enjoying a moment of a lifetime. We hugged and we congratulated each other. We were both so, so happy.

But we could not stay there for long. The midday mass for pilgrims was just about to begin. So we practically ran through the Rua de San Francisco, the street that connects the Obradoiro square and the San Francisco church, and entered the church just at the moment as the priest and his entourage walked down the aisle of the main nave singing a holy song.

The church was packed. There were not just no seats left, it was also hard to find a standing place. We split and I went to the right-side aisle to find a priest for a confession. There were many lines for confession, and I stepped in one of them and waited. As it was my turn it turned out the priest only spoke Spanish, so he sent me to the opposite side aisle where there was an English speaking priest. Luckily his line was not long. There were just two pilgrims in front of me. Each of them took maybe just two or three minutes of confessor's time. It was the same with me. Since I missed two Sunday masses on my one-month journey to Santiago de Compostela, the penance he gave me was mild but a lasting one- to speak and spread my experience of the Camino.

Confession done I returned to the right aisle where I left my backpack leaned on one of the church pillars. Mass went on with all of us pilgrims being more than happy to be there. Then it was time for communion. We all stepped in lines, the whole church singing. It took time. There were so many people there. As I received Corpus Christi, I returned to the same spot as before. There it happened again. All the emotions erupted. It was actually at that very moment that all came on me. I broke down in tears. Tears of happiness and gratitude, that I made it. That I haven't failed. And that it was His will to lead me safely all the way here.

As I started my journey one month ago, I was full of doubts. I was 50 years old and I was not sure if I would be able to do the Camino. I feared that I might injure my ankle or my knee. I feared I might get ill and stay in bed. I feared I might get robbed (I must say that on none of my journeys I felt so safe as I felt on the Camino), I feared that I might simply crush and quit. But none of that happened. All turned out OK and I was here at the end of my pilgrimage in Santiago de Compostela in the church at the pilgrim's midday mass. And I was totally overwhelmed by the feelings. Crying tears of happiness. Though this time as I sensed it coming, I didn't fight it, as back in Sahagun. I just let it go. This time I already knew, this is a normal part of the Camino experience - "Everybody cries on the Camino!" So as it was over, it didn't drain me out, as when it happened to me for the first time.

Mass was coming to an end, so I stood up and looked around to see where Bjorn is. Instead of finding him I saw some other familiar faces, so I went to greet them. I found Bjorn only after exiting the Church. But not just him I also found my dear friend Paul. I introduced him to Bjorn and all three of us went to the pilgrim's office. Paul led the way since he was already there a few hours earlier. He has already got his Compostela certificate. On our way there we agreed that after picking the certificate for Bjorn and me, we would go for lunch together.

The line in the pilgrim's office was very long so it took us more than an hour to get our Compostelas. But it was worth waiting. It is a unique document that confirms the accomplishment. Later on I have learned that in many countries it is taken as one of the highly valuable documents at various contests. If you apply for a job in Spain it shows the employer that you are a person that will do the job no matter the obstacles. In South Korea it brings extra points to future students as they try to get a place at preferred universities. Paul waited patiently for the two of us in the pilgrims office inner garden. There at the fountain he took a picture of me with the document I just received. Then we went together for lunch.

We picked one of the places in the narrow city streets. There are many since Santiago de Compostela is a big city and many pilgrims come there every day. And they all have to eat. We ordered three main dishes and three large beers. As we were served, we first toasted on our accomplishments. It was a special toast especially for Paul since this was his first beer after a month. Then we said a prayer and started to eat. My main dish was the shells of Saint James. Yes, definitely something I was determined to treat myself with if I managed to come here. They were delicious. We stayed there and talked for like an hour and then we had to go, each of us to find our hostels. We parted with a hug and a traditional Buen Camino. This was the last time I saw both of them.

My hotel was near the city central bus station. On the same side of the street. Maybe just 100 meters away from it. It was an apartment on the 3rd floor. I made a reservation for it over Booking.com. The hosteliero welcomed me, gave me the keys and showed me my bed. It was in a small room with only two bunks. Only one lower bed was occupied, and I got the other lower one. I took a shower, changed my clothes and went back to town.

Now it was time to visit the cathedral. On my way there I called my Italian friends and we agreed to meet for dinner at 9 pm. Cathedral was under renovation, but it was still possible to visit the grave of the saint. Since it was already 7pm as I got there, there were not many people inside. First, I climbed the stairs up to the saint's statue and gave Saint James a long hug. It is a tradition for the pilgrims, to thank him that way, for his protection on the pilgrimage. During that hug one of my thoughts was also with the old lady that helped me to find the way in Calzada del Coto.Then I went down to the crypt. In the crypt it is usual to say a prayer. I said many. Not just for myself, but also for the people I did my walks for, during my days on the Camino. It was my decision from the very beginning to dedicate every day of my walking to someone. The first days in the Pyrenees were dedicated to my family. First day I dedicated to the two of us - my wife and me. Then the next three days to my daughters. And the next one to my parents. Later on I walked for my friends. Last two days of my walking were dedicated to my ancestors. Yesterday I walked for all the members of my family on my mother's side. And today – on my last day of walking – I walked for all the members of my family on my father's side. Especially for his father – my grandfather – whose name was Jakob (James in English and Yago in Spanish). Walking for my grandfather James on the last day was a special gesture to bound my pilgrimage with my whole family. A symbolic bond, especially since during the time I was on my Camino, exactly 70 years have passed from his early death - being only 49 years old.

I never knew him but my father told me a lot about him. I am sure my grandfather James has followed me on my way to Santiago de Compostela from above and I am proud to write the Camino pilgrimage into our family's history.

When I finished all the prayers for my family and friends I got up from my knees and exited the script. It was almost 8 pm so I left the cathedral.

As I arrived at the restaurant my Italian friends, Alessia and Massimo, were already there. They came to Santiago de Compostela this afternoon and also already got their Compostela. For the pilgrims mass it was their plan to attend it tomorrow. We had a great dinner and a great conversation. I felt Italian language was no longer an obstacle. Looks like we found that minimal amount of words that I managed to speak and understand so we were able to communicate freely. Of course there were still some moments where uncle Google helped us a great deal.

After dinner it was time for goodbye. This was the last time I saw Alessia and Massimo. They invited me to visit their town after our return back home but I haven't found the time yet. It is like with many other encounters. As the river of time flows on, they slowly fade away.

Coming to the hostel I saw everyone was already asleep. So was I a minute later.

Toward Finistere

As I opened my eyes the girl across the room was already packing. After mutual good mornings we introduced ourselves. Her name was Sarah. As I started to pack my stuff, she told me she is leaving Santiago de Compostela today. She returned from Finistere yesterday and she was about to go to Madrid today and later return back to Germany. As I was ready to go, she asked me if I am for a cup of coffee before I go. It was a great idea, so we went to the hostel's kitchen. She made a great filter coffee, and I found some cereal for breakfast. After we finished our breakfast, I thanked her for the delicious coffee and wished her: "Buen Camino!". Ten minutes later I was on the street and twenty minutes later I was on the Praza do Obradoiro. One last look at the cathedral and then on toward the Finistere.

I left the Obradoiro down the right path that goes in front of the hotel Parador. On the bottom of the slope the Camino goes through a city street. There, not more than 100 meters from Praza do Obradoiro, I met another pilgrim. I asked him if he is also going to Finistere and he replied that he is. His name was Mathias. He was from Germany so we spoke German. Just like me, he came to Santiago de Compostela yesterday. The difference was that he has made the most challenging Camino - the Camino Norte and that he has started his journey in France in Bordeaux.

It was nice to have someone to talk to. We walked together for like an hour and then stopped for a small meal. After that we parted since he was a much faster walker and I was not able to follow his tempo. I walked alone for the rest of the day.

Today it was Monday and it was my first day of walking after I finished my pilgrimage in Santiago de Compostela. I was happy to have had enough time to go to Finistere before I had to go back home. My flight was on Friday morning and I only needed 3 days to go to the end of the world. I will be there on Wednesday. I wanted to go to Finistere not just to make 800+ kilometres but also because I wanted to finish my pilgrimage in a traditional way. Centuries ago there were no written confirmations issued to the pilgrims that came to Santiago de Compostela. The only proof was the Saint James shell that you brought back home. But to get a shell you had to go to the ocean beaches of Galicia and pick one up.

It was also my first day of social media silence. I was posting all my days from Saint Jean Pied de Port to Santiago de Compostela, but I wanted to have those three days just for myself. To enjoy my success and to sort out all the thoughts in my head.

At 4.30 pm I came to the bridge over river Tambre in the Ponte Maceira village. It is another Roman bridge you pass on the Camino. I must admit it is also one of the most scenic ones. There I met two pilgrims Maria and Kliment. We just said hello since we were all so preoccupied with taking pictures of a beautiful bridge and its surroundings.

The largest town I passed that day was Negreira. I came there late in the afternoon and it was hot as hell. At 6 pm the thermometer still showed 91°F (33°C). But by now this was not a problem for me any more. I was well walked in and just getting a drink there was enough to walk on. My plan was to walk beyond 30 kilometres that day and I did.

I came to a small hostel – Albergue O Rueiro in Vilaserio at sunset. It was between 9.30 and 10pm. I was late but it was no problem, in the hostel they knew I would be coming late. They gave me the bed and I got dinner. We spoke over the phone twice during the day. My first call was about the reservation and my second was from Negreira telling them I will be late.

I actually learned about the hostel already in the morning since I saw advertising boards for it along the way. On the first board it was unfortunately not possible to read the telephone number, so I had to wait until the next one to get the number, and then call them and make a reservation. I told the owner about their first board and showed him the picture where it was clearly visible that someone had partially destroyed the table, so that the phone number was not visible. He was shocked. He didn't know about that, but he appreciated the information very much. He thanked me for it with a desert on his account.

Energy of the Camino

Tuesday was the middle day on my way from Santiago de Compostela to Finisterre. The destination goal that day was a little village called Hospital.

I started my walk at 9 am. Around midday I met an old man who was walking the same path. He was 79 years old. Practically the age of my father who is 80.

I couldn't believe that he was walking the Camino at that age, since my father can nowadays only do just a couple of steps. But here it was this old guy walking the Camino toward the Finistare. And not just that, after a couple of kilometres I figured it out, that the old man is actually walking faster than me. I was impressed!

At 3 pm we met Maria. She was setting her tent in one of the fields. We joked that this living room she just chose has a great view. An hour later, at 4pm the old man announced he had had enough for that day, so we parted.

For the next hour I walked alone. At 5 pm I stopped at a pub in A Ponte Olveiroa for a small snack and a glass of beer. There I met Klimt again. We sat and ate there for 30 minutes but then I had to go on. As I understand it he stayed there for the night.

At 6 pm I was shortly before Olveiroa and there it happened again. This time it was the last such experience on my Camino. For good or for worse. I do not now, but I guess I got all of my lectures.

I was walking on the road and all of the sudden I noticed an old man. He has been standing at the other side of the street holding a wooden stick with both hands in front of him. He stood there completely still.

Already back after my meeting with the gypsies in Santa Irene, I made a decision that the next time something like that happens to me I will shake hands with the person, so that I will make sure that he is really there in flesh and blood.

So this time I was determined to shake hands with the old men. I crossed the road and walked straight to him.

By that time I was already a confirmed pilgrim. I have got my Compostela certificate in the pilgrims office in Santiago de Compostela. I attended the pilgrim's mass. I prayed on the grave of the saint. I was full of faith and full of Christ. I was a totally holy person. But was I really?

As I was just five steps from the old man I greeted him with the usual: "Buenas tardes!" And as I was maybe just two or three steps away; just as I almost stretched my hand to offer a hand shake something unbelievable happened.

The old man opened his mouth and started to drool. A stream of saliva started to flow from his mouth just like a waterfall. It flew over his hands still helding the stick in front of him. In an instant his hands were totally covered with saliva.

This disgusted me, and as I was just a step away I didn't offer him my hand. At that moment he lifted his right hand and put his stretched index finger to his lips. He showed me to shut up.

I didn't say anything. I just passed him.

As I was 3 or 4 steps away, it became all totally clear to me. I have failed the test.

I have disowned Jesus. If I was really all holy, I should have not just shook hands with the man, I should have embraced him. Give him a hug. I saw the command two hours ago: "Hoy te regalo mis abrazos ☺" (Today I am donating you my hugs.). I should have shown him all the christian love. I was ashamed but it was already too late.

The lesson taught me that no matter what I have achieved I am still just an ordinary human being. A man who will fall many times under the burden of his cross. A man that will deny Jesus through his actions no matter how determined to love him. A man with all his mistakes. An average person. Nothing special. As far as possible from being holy.

It was a bitter recognition. But I have to live with it. I guess this is how we all are. Far from perfect.

MM on my stick was there for a reason. My friend Miha, who made the stick, was an old fox. He knew human nature and he cut those letters of "Memento mori" there as a prophecy. With a good reason. I was not modest enough as I finished my Camino, and I got a lesson directly from God.

I had a couple of hours to think about it all since after I passed Olveiroa I was on a mountain path again. Walking through a beautiful landscape up on the slopes of the river valley. The river down in the valley shone in the afternoon sun reflecting its rays. Nature was really magnificent. So beautiful as if it was telling me : "Look I honour God with all of the beauty he gave me with his creation. How about you? How do you honour God?" A little bit of extra salt on my wounds. I deserved it for being so full of pride.

I came to Hospital at 8 pm. The village was completely empty. Information office was closed. No person was to be seen. There was just a white dog. A big beast. Not in a friendly mood. He sat there at the road and snarled at me.

I was totally in a repellent mood so I thought to myself. What a hell. If it is meant for him to bite me then let it be. So I stopped there in front of him. The dog stood up and started to bark at me.

I took down my backpack and pulled out a package of prosciutto. I took one slice of prosciutto out of the package and squatted down a meter and a half from the dog. Holding the prosciutto in my palm I stretched my hand toward the dog. At that moment the beast already totally lost its mind. It was jumping around and snarling and barking at me. I didn't know what was going to happen. I was ready for anything. I let it be in God's hands.

I guess His judgement was that I got enough lessons for the day. The dog lowered himself down and started slowly approaching me. He has smelled the prosciutto but was not sure about me. I just kept my position and waited. He started to calm down. He barked just here and there and mowed zigzagging toward me. Still hesitating either to trust me either not. But the prosciutto did the job. He overcame his fear. He grabbed the dried meat from my hand and jumped away.

He ate the slice and started to wave his tail. He was satisfied with the taste, and he was satisfied with me. He saw I had no intention of harming him. Four slices later we were already big friends.

The whole event with this beast reminded me of a story a friend of mine told me long ago. It is a well-known story about two wolfs. The story goes that everybody has in their soul two wolfs. One is good the other is bad. The usual narrative is that if you want to be a good person you should only feed the good one. I advocated for that same solution for years, but then the life experiences taught me that you should actually be nice to both wolfs and feed them both. By doing so, you first are not discriminative toward any of the wolfs and second – since we are speaking about the parts of our souls - it is important to be aware of our shadow side. Only by knowing our shadow we can admit we have a problem and start working on it. And on top of everything - speaking of the two wolfs- if both of them are your friends, you can always count that it is going to be the wild one that will help you save yourself when faced with a critical life threatening situation. So always feed the beasts no matter how dangerously they look. The raven is always a friend of the wolf.

The hostel in Hospital is at the end of the village. Actually there is the pub where you have dinner and later they take you to the centre of the village, to the dormitory.

I entered the pub and found a spare table. It was a small dining room with not more than four tables. One was occupied with four girls from the USA and the other with a married couple of my age. The two of them were also from the USA. While I was eating the girls left the room.

After I finished my supper and was just sitting there enjoying the wine we started a conversation. The usual stuff. Where the two of them are from, how long are they on the Camino, etc. A relaxed after dinner conversation.

Then the lady asked me what in my opinion is the most important thing of the Camino? I have been thinking about that many times in my days on the Camino. There were so many different dimensions. All of them interlocked. It was hard to decide which component was the most important. It took me many days to carefully weigh them and put them in ranks. But by then as I was asked my opinion was already clear.

And I told her: "It is the people. They are the most important part of the Camino. They would be the reason for me to come back. I admire how nice they all are to one another. I admire their willingness to help. They are all so positive. No wonder the Camino fills you with such a positive energy. It is really unique. There is nothing like it. It really is a holy place full of positive energy. And it is such because of the people – the pilgrims."

Then I asked her: "What is the name of that famous concert that you had in the USA fifty years ago?"

She replied: "You mean Woodstock?"

I continued: " Yes exactly! You remember it. The concert lasted just for three days but the young people from all parts of the USA gathered there for the whole week. And all of those young people were full of positive energy. Positive energy toward one another, positive energy toward the whole society and positive energy toward nature. And in the next 50 years that positive energy, from only one week of Woodstock, transformed the US completely. It was the effect of the positive energy of only one week! And here on the Camino, you have positive people walking it every day, 365 days, 52 week per year for more than 10 centuries. Here you have a constant flow of positive energy for more than a thousand years. Can you Imagine what this enormous amount of positive energy is doing to the world? It is unbelievable."

As I looked at her, she stared at me with her eyes wide open. She was shocked. She was speechless. The only thing she was able to say was: "What a metaphor."

After that we remained silent. Each of us deep within our thoughts. There was really not much more to be added.

I paid my bill and the lady of the house took me to the dormitory in the centre of the village. The dormitory was nothing special. A sort of kitchen on the ground level and a room full of bunks on the first floor. I came as last and got the last upper bed. After a quick shower the sleep came in no time.

My final steps on the Camino were into the ocean

Wednesday the 15th of May 2019 was my last day of walking. I was about 30 kilometres from Finistere as I started my day.

The day started with a drama since the girls that I met at the beginning of yesterday's dinner split after a hard quarrel they have had yesterday evening. The quarrel took place after they left the pub and came to the dormitory. This morning the three of them left the fourth one alone here in the dormitory. And she was sitting at her bed crying.

I asked her what happened and she explained to me that she was the leader of the group. Their guide. I learned that they are all students. They started their Camino in Finistere yesterday and the problem was that the road was too hard for them. They have imagined the pilgrimage in a more romantic way. They haven't expected it to be so physically challenging. The girls that left that morning all blamed her for walking such a long distance on the first day, for walking uphill practically the whole afternoon and on top of all for once choosing the wrong way. This was the first time she was here and it was also the first time she acted as a guide.

Meanwhile, as she was talking to me, she managed to stand up from her bed and started to pack. When she finished talking and packing I didn't know what to say. I am not good at such emotional things. At least her tears stopped. It looked like her talking and my listening helped a little bit. I tried to comfort her by saying it will all sort out. But she didn't believe me. Neither was I. So I just gave her a sincere comforting hug and then we parted with a traditional "Buen Camino". At least those two words brought a brief smile to her face. I guess at that moment she got that first feeling of being a part of the pilgrimage family. She had just started her journey yesterday and I was finishing mine today. The contrast between our situations could not be bigger. But I remembered my first days. They were not easy. So I understood that yesterday it must have been really hard for her. But after all, today was another day.

Outside the sun was coming through the clouds and at 9 am I was already out of Hospital.

Five minutes later I came to the famous crossroad (it is actually a roundabout) with two milestones. One for the direction toward Finisterre the other one for the direction toward Muxia. I took a selfie and followed the first direction.

I came to the hills overlooking the coastal town of Cee at 11.30 am. There on my way down the slope road, as the morning bay fog started to disintegrate under the power of the zenith approaching sun, it was finally the time to catch the first glimpses of the ocean. The view was still foggy but my eyes caught the first silhouettes of the boats down in the harbor. At 1 pm I was in Cee. I have reached the ocean, but I was still a couple of hours from Finistere.

On my way there Helmut called and told me that he and the rest of my German speaking friends came to Santiago de Compostela this morning. He then asked me where I am and I explained to him that I will be in Finistere this afternoon. He congratulated me on my accomplishment and then we said goodbye.

I came to Finistere at 4 pm. I went to the beach, took off my shoes and walked into the water. My final steps on the Camino were into the ocean. I came to the end of the world. I have made 800+ kilometres and it felt great. This was the symbolic ending of my month of walking.

Exiting the water I was no longer a pilgrim but just a tourist.

I picked up my backpack that was lying on the beach sand and went to the showers nearby to wash all the beach sand from my feet and to put back my shoes. With my shoes back on I went to the center of the Finistere.

There is a little path that ascends from the beach up into the town. As I came up that path I saw a cross. And there at the cross I saw a man I haven't seen for weeks. It was Helmut. He was there waiting for me. He was smiling. I couldn't believe my eyes.

He congratulated me for finishing my Camino here in Finistere with a handshake and a big hug. Helmut, Pascal and Martin have come here to surprise me. It was an act of true friendship. Another proof of the positive energy of the people that walk the Camino. I was totally impressed.

Unfortunately I was so late that Pascal must have left since he had to catch the late night bus from Santiago de Compostela back home. This was really a pity. It would be nice to see him on my last day since he was one of the first pilgrims I met on my first day on the Camino, when I was ascending the Pyrenees mountains from Saint Jack Pied de Port on Palm Sunday four and a half weeks back.

But Martin was in the hotel waiting for me and Helmut to show up. On our way toward the hotel Helmut took my backpack. He said that this is another symbolic act of friendship – to help a friend to carry his burden for at least a little part of his way.

I was really glad to see Martin again. We always had a great chemistry in those first days on the Camino as we were still walking together. He will always remain in my memories as one of the most positive people I met. Modest, mostly silent, always smiling while talking and most of all very much on the same frequency of thinking as myself. I was really so glad to see him again.

We set a time for dinner but I had two more things to do. First I picked up my last certificate – the one that said I came all the way to Finisterre. Second I had to go to the end of the Finistere peninsula – to the famous lighthouse. The lighthouse is "just" three kilometres from town. Without a backpack (I left it in my hotel room) I was there in no time.

One more fortunate encounter happened on my way to the lighthouse. For days I have been following a South Korean couple on Instagram. Their posts were really great. I liked that great sense of aesthetics on the photos they have posted. And there on my way toward the lighthouse they came the other way. They have been there and were now on their way back to Finistere. I stopped them and explained to them my admiration of their photos. They said that they have also followed my posts and that they are really happy to meet me in person. We made a selfie together and our smiles tell it all.

0,000 km stone is a special stone. Just like the 100,00 km stone it is one of the most photographed stones on the Camino. It stands just a couple of meters from the lighthouse. As I came there it was already late afternoon. There weren't many people there. Weather was a little bit cloudy but the daylight was still strong. It was still nice to look toward the sea horizon.

I have left my backpack in the hotel room but I brought with me two things. The first one was my stick. I have managed to bring it all the way to the end of the world. It was not an easy task so I was quite proud about that accomplishment. It was long and heavy but it also brought me lots of joy. I knew that the next challenge would be to bring it home.

The second thing was a little candy. The one that Tess left me on the bed in Zubiri as she gave me her bed and went to sleep on the couch. I kept it carefully all the way here to Finistere. For me it was like some kind of lucky charm. It reminded me how lucky I was to get a bed that rainy night in Zubiry a month ago. Tess was really an angel. As I came back home I sent her the candy, a bottle of wine and a letter of thanks for all of her kindness.

Dinner with Helmut and Martin was at 8 pm. We were no longer pilgrims. Now we were tourists so we acted like ones. We went to the harbor. There we found a good sea pub and ordered large plates of seafood. We had so many things to discuss so the hours just flew by. It is really unbelievable how time flies if you are in a good company. I was also very glad to see that Giovana was sitting at the neighbouring table. I haven't seen her for days. I didn't want to disturb her too much since she was not alone so I just went there to give her a brief hello. She was glad to see me and as her group was leaving she brought me her piece of chocolate cake. It was a nice gesture and the cake was delicious.

We finished our dinner very late. We were among the last guests leaving the pub. As we came back to our hotel it was almost midnight. We agreed to meet in the morning for breakfast and then to catch the bus back to Santiago de Compostela.

It was a perfect day with a perfect ending.

Last day in Santiago de Compostela

It is unbelievable how quickly the bus comes from Finisterre to Santiago de Compostela. What took me three days of walking, takes only an hour of driving by bus. It was really a funny feeling. Not just to travel so fast but also the very feeling of driving in a bus. It was after all my first drive after a month and I needed some time to adjust.

The bus was full. We were all three on the bus - Helmut, Martin and I. I saw Giovana was also on the same bus. As we came to Santiago de Compostela she joined us on our way to the nearest hostel. Helmut knew about one that was just newly opened so we all followed him.

Hostel was really just opened. It operated for not more than a month. I saw it from the list of guests that there were really not many there yet. I for example was only the fourth person from Slovenia that came there. The owner also encouraged us to help him with the decoration of the walls. His idea was to let pilgrims make their inscriptions there. Some had already put their signatures there; others had painted some pictures. We did both after we put our backpacks in the rooms and were there in the dining room preparing to drink a cup of coffee.

As we were in the middle of our painting and coffee drinking another familiar face entered. It was Matthias from Germany.

Then it was time to go to town. We all had different plans so we agreed to meet for dinner at 6 pm in a pub in the centre of the old town. Not far away from the cathedral.

After another meeting with friends, in front of the cathedral, I went shopping since a father of three daughters could not come home empty handed. I got three blue hoodies with a yellow Compostela arrow in front. A perfect gift since they were all proud users of the hoodies with their schools logos.

I also had to buy some little souvenirs for all of my friends that have followed me on social media and supported me in my hardest moments on the Camino. I found the same kind of wristbands like the one I bought in San Miguel del Camino - the one that I still wear.

After I did the shopping I went to the cathedral again. I wanted to say some more prayers on the grave of the Saint. After exiting the script and walking around the cathedral I met Giovana. She was also there to do her prayers. As we exited, we went for a coffee in a little canteen just opposite the side entrance to the cathedral.

At 4 pm I was back in the hostel and I packed my shopping items into my backpack. Luckily I had enough space in my backpack, besides now it was no longer necessary to watch how much it weighs. Now it will be carried by means of transportation and not by my shoulders.

At 6pm we were in the pub. It was not just Helmut, Martin, Giovana and me, but also all of the other friends from my German speaking group and many of their friends they met later on the Camino. I was very happy I saw Jana again. She hasn't walked with the rest of the group. She decided to walk alone just like me and was always just shortly behind me on the Camino. Maybe just a day or a couple of hours away. We were in contact via social media a couple of times but never managed to meet on the Camino. Now we finally managed to see each other again.

We got a large table in the pub. I was glad Helmut made a reservation since it was pretty crowded. We all had a lot to talk about and many reasons for toasts. We were all so happy we had made it successfully to Santiago de Compostela and we were even more happy to be together again.

And as we were there sitting, eating and celebrating our successes, another, to me very dear person, entered the pub. It was Richard. Richard my friend. The one I first met at breakfast in Roncesvalles. The one I met with his friends as I entered Pamplona. The one I met with his friends later at the pilgrims monument on Alto the Perdon, where I told them the story of my pilgrim's staff after which the girl with the pearl earrings named Lucia asked if it is allowed to touch it. The one I met then for the last time in Najera. And not least, the one I was also constantly in contact with on social media and constantly hoped I would meet for one last time at the end of the road. And now here he was. We gave each other a great, strong hug. It was a kind of God's will that we meet again. He and his friend might have chosen some other pub and we would never meet. It was perfect. He and his friends joined our table. Now the table was practically through the whole pub long. Luckily the owners of the pub understood those feelings and made no problems. Of course we gave them a great tip at the end.

After we finished our dinner we went for another glass of beer. We sat in a garden of the nearby bar. By then it was already a little bit cold outside so we didn't stay long.

Then it was time for our last goodbyes. I was glad I had the opportunity to meet Jana and Richard for one last time that evening. We parted with a promise to keep in touch via social media.

When our small group, Helmut, Martin, Giovana and I, came to our hostel I just took a shower and went to bed. It was already almost midnight and I had to get up early tomorrow to catch my plane.

Epilogue

It was really nice to come back home and be with the family after 5 weeks. I came back on Friday evening (May 16th) and it was magic. Family was overwhelmed with emotions. My wife remarked that it is not only that I have lost 10 kilos, but that it looks like I've also lost 10 years – that I look much younger.

On Saturday we went to celebrate my friend's 50th birthday and on Sunday we rested for the whole day.

I really needed a rest. A lot of rest. Only in the second week of my return I kind of feel I am 95% OK. First days at home were really interesting. After 5 weeks of constant everyday walking you physically feel kind of lost. Your body is confused. I noticed that I had no appetite in the first days since my body has not given me any signals that I need any extra food. I think my body felt like there was no need for energy intake since there was no energy spent on walking. It was really strange. I remember that I felt trembling from some kind of unexplainable cold in the bed in the evening and had been woken up a couple of hours later completely wet from intense sweating. Thermoregulation of my body was a total mess. This went on for like 4 to 5 days. On Monday (May 20th) I already went to work and started the old daily routine. Breakfast, drive to work, work, break for lunch, drive back home, early supper, evening snack and all this brought me back to normal. I also remember how thirsty I was for the first few days. My body needed a lot of liquid - water, juice,... I was kind of deeply dehydrated.

The other very intense part of my return were the meetings with all the people here in Slovenia that have followed me on social media throughout the time I was on Camino. We all felt some strangely strong bond. Those meetings were magic. All the congratulations, all the hand shakes, all the hugs. Wonderful! What an energy. I spent hours of the afternoons and evenings with friends talking about the experiences of the Camino - memory still completely fresh.

Camino was really an unique experience. All that energy of the people that I have met. All pilgrims that were so positive, willing to help and open to share. I especially like how equal all the people are on the Camino. It is not important who you are or what you are. Pilgrims only ask you for the name, so that they know how to call you, and where you are from, so that they approximately know in which language they can talk to you. Nothing else matters. On Camino you are just a pilgrim. I really appreciate that feeling. And I highly respect that attitude. It is definitely one of the things that will stay in my memory forever and one of the reasons I am sure I will return to Camino someday. Camino was definitely 100 times more of what I have ever expected.

One year later (2020)

What an adventure this Camino was! After more than a year I am still completely taken over by the experience. My friend Matej told me that there is a saying: »You walk on the Camino for a month and than the Camino walks on you for many months.« It is 100% true.

In the summer of 2020, as the COVID19 epidemics gave us a little break, I asked Miha, my pilgrim's staff maker, to take me to the place where he cut the tree for the staff. So he, Matej and I sat in his car and he took us up toward the church of St. Primus above Kamnik.

The location where he cut the trunk for my pilgrim's stick is above the road on a forest slope between two mountain streams, no more than 200 meters from the church of St. Primus. One part of the tree is still there. On that tree I have tied the St. James shell that I brought back from Santiago de Compostela. A piece of wood from this very location has followed me all the way to Finistere and back. And to bring back a shell from Spanish Galicia back here, was my way to close the full circle.

And completing the circles is important. In 1899, the German poet Reiner Marija Rilke wrote: "Ich lebe mein Leben in wachsenden Ringen" or: "I live my life in growing circles."

Regardless of all the advances in science and technology, some fundamental insights about the life always remain the same – even after more than one hundred. One of these realizations is that through all our lives we constantly move around the same circles.

The first and most important is our family circle, then there are the circles of our friends, the circle of colleagues, the circle of our neighbours and a number of other circles. Some circles are longer, some shorter. Some of them we drawn only once. Some of them we repeat all of the times. We enter many circles not to even be aware of them. But regardless of the length of the circumference, we always return to the same starting points. It is in the nature of the universe to close the circles – just think about the planets.

There is but one special circle. The longest one. The circle of our life. We come from God and we go back to Him.

Many people we knew are no longer with us. They have completed their circles. Age, illness, accidents and hardships have taken them away for good. Someday we will meet them again in a circle that never closes - in a circle whose circumference is a straight line – in the circle of eternity.

Four years later (2023)

After 4 years I came back to the Camino for 4 days. Last +100 km. Saria - Santiago de Compostela. It is still as magic as it was. I miss you all my dear 2019 Camino friends!

Greetings from Camino!

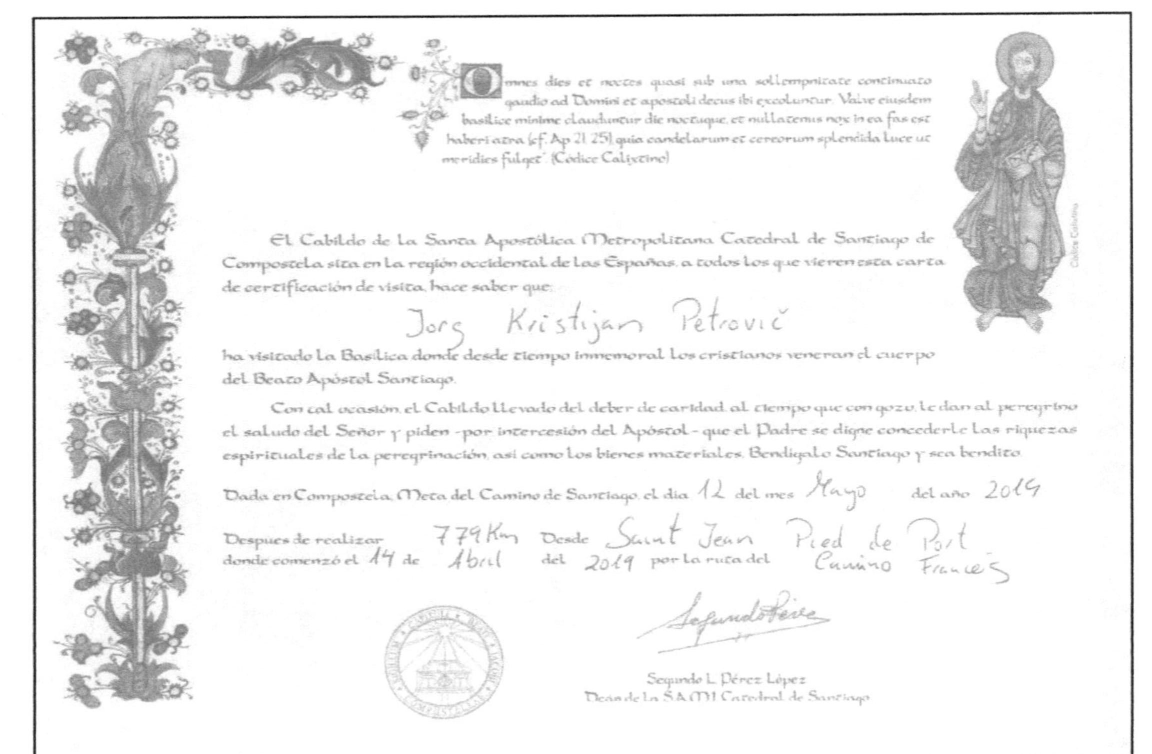

"Omnes dies et noctes quasi sub una sollempnitate continuato gaudio ad Domini et apostoli decus ibi excoluntur. Valve eiusdem basilice minime clauduntur die noctuque, et nullatenus nox in ea fas est haberi atra (cf. Ap 21 25), quia candelarum et cereorum splendida luce ut meridies fulget". (Códice Calixtino)

El Cabildo de la Santa Apostólica Metropolitana Catedral de Santiago de Compostela sita en la región occidental de las Españas, a todos los que vieren esta carta de certificación de visita, hace saber que:

Jorg Kristijan Petrović

ha visitado la Basílica donde desde tiempo inmemoral los cristianos veneran el cuerpo del Beato Apóstol Santiago.

Con tal ocasión, el Cabildo llevado del deber de caridad, al tiempo que con gozo, le dan al peregrino el saludo del Señor y piden -por intercesión del Apóstol- que el Padre se digne concederle las riquezas espirituales de la peregrinación, así como los bienes materiales. Bendígalo Santiago y sea bendito.

Dada en Compostela, Meta del Camino de Santiago, el día 12 del mes Mayo del año 2019

Después de realizar 779 Km Desde Saint Jean Pied de Port donde comenzó el 14 de Abril del 2019 por la ruta del Camino Francés

Segundo L. Pérez López
Deán de la S.A.M.I. Catedral de Santiago

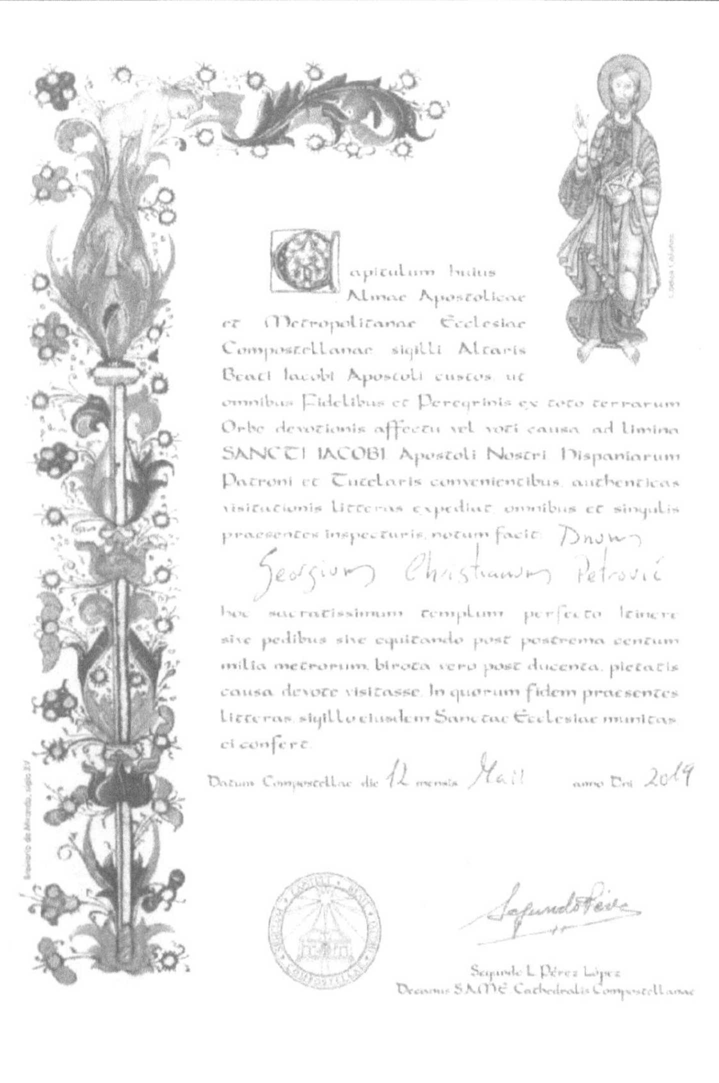

Capitulum huius Almae Apostolicae et Metropolitanae Ecclesiae Compostellanae sigilli Altaris Beati Iacobi Apostoli custos, ut omnibus Fidelibus et Peregrinis ex toto terrarum Orbe devotionis affectu vel voti causa ad limina SANCTI IACOBI Apostoli Nostri Hispaniarum Patroni et Tutelaris convenientibus, authenticas visitationis litteras expediat, omnibus et singulis praesentes inspecturis, notum facit: Dnum

Georgium Christianum Petrović

hoc sacratissimum templum perfecto itinere sive pedibus sive equitando post postrema centum milia metrorum, birota vero post ducenta, pietatis causa devote visitasse. In quorum fidem praesentes litteras, sigillo eiusdem Sanctae Ecclesiae munitas, ei confert.

Datum Compostellae die 12 mensis Maii anno Dni 2019

Sejundo L. Pérez López
Decanus S.A.M.E. Cathedralis Compostellanae

epan cuantos esta Carta Peregrina vieren como

Jorg Kristijan Petrovic

ha pasado por tierras leonesas de Sahagún,
Centro Geográfico del Camino de Santiago francés y como
reza en el Codex Calixtinus "... pródigo en todo tipo de bienes,
donde se encuentra el prado, en el que se dice, antaño
reverdecieron las astas fulgurantes que los guerreros
victoriosos habían hincado en tierra, para gloria del Señor".
Y que según atestigua, ha encontrado reposo para las fatigas
del cuerpo y alivio de las almas.

os moradores de esta noble villa le damos ánimos
para seguir su camino y llegar con buena andanza a la casa del
Señor Santiago, donde esperamos tenga un recuerdo de los
que le hemos dado acogida.

para que conste y pueda ser exhibida ante quien se lo
demande, firmo la presente en

Sahagún, a 28 de **Abril** del año del Señor de 2019

El Alcalde.

Lisandro García de la Viuda

Carta Peregrina 24825

O Concello de Fisterra acredita que
Jons Kristijan Petrović
chegou a estas terras da Costa da Morte
e fin do Camiño Xacobeo
Fisterra 15/5/2019   O Alcalde
862 Km.

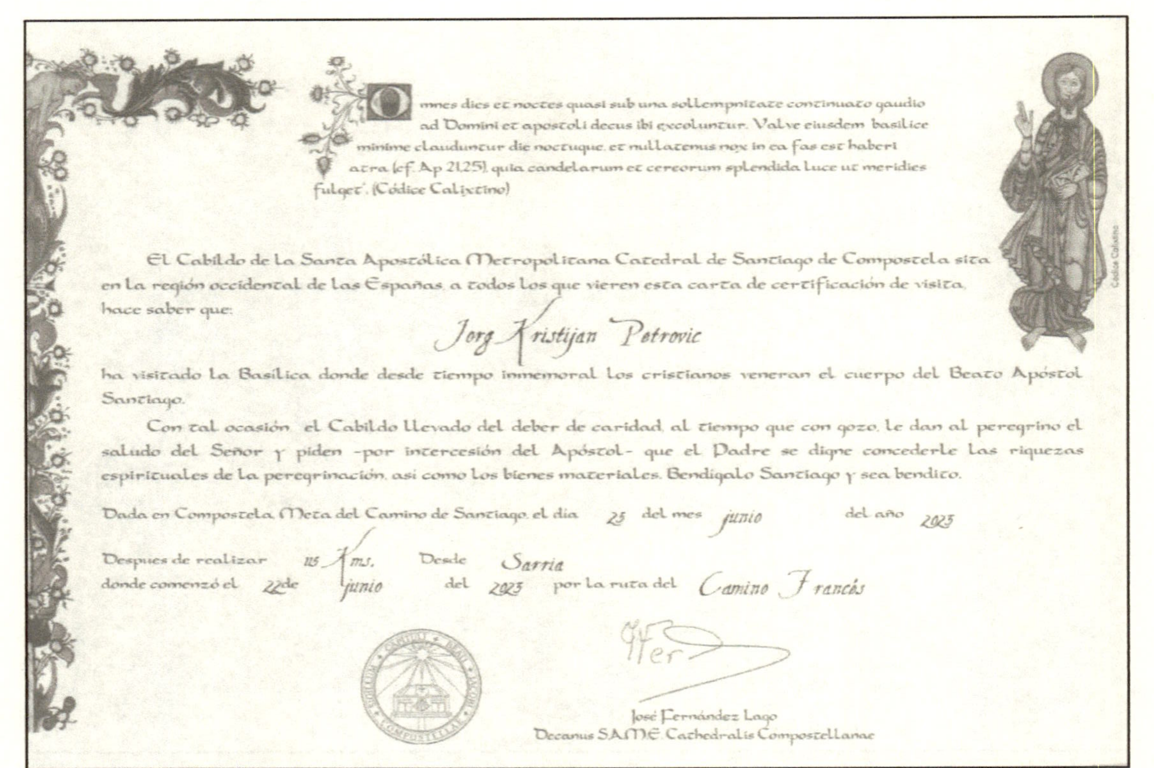

Omnes dies et noctes quasi sub una sollempnitate continuato gaudio
ad Domini et apostoli decus ibi excoluntur. Valve eiusdem basilice
minime clauduntur die noctuque, et nullatenus nox in ea fas est haberi
atra (cf. Ap 21,25), quia candelarum et cereorum splendida luce ut meridies
fulget'. (Códice Calixtino)

El Cabildo de la Santa Apostólica Metropolitana Catedral de Santiago de Compostela sita
en la región occidental de las Españas, a todos los que vieren esta carta de certificación de visita,
hace saber que:

Jorg Kristijan Petrovic

ha visitado la Basílica donde desde tiempo inmemoral los cristianos veneran el cuerpo del Beato Apóstol
Santiago.

Con tal ocasión, el Cabildo llevado del deber de caridad, al tiempo que con gozo, le dan al peregrino el
saludo del Señor y piden -por intercesión del Apóstol- que el Padre se digne concederle las riquezas
espirituales de la peregrinación, así como los bienes materiales. Bendígalo Santiago y sea bendito.

Dada en Compostela Meta del Camino de Santiago, el día 25 del mes junio del año 2023

Despues de realizar 115 Kms. Desde Sarria
donde comenzó el 22 de junio del 2023 por la ruta del Camino Francés

José Fernández Lago
Decanus SAME Cathedralis Compostellanae

Códice Calixtino

Capitulum huius Almae Apostolicae et Metropolitanae Ecclesiae Compostellanae, sigilli Altaris Beati Iacobi Apostoli custos ut omnibus Fidelibus et Peregrinis ex toto terrarum Orbe, devotionis affectu vel voti causa, ad Limina SANCTI IACOBI, Apostoli Nostri, Hispaniarum Patroni et Tutelaris convenientibus, authenticas visitationis litteras expediat, omnibus et singulis praesentes inspecturis, notum facit: Dominum

Jorg Kristijan Petrovic

hoc sacratissimum templum, perfecto Itinere sive pedibus sive equitando post postrema centum milia metrorum, birota vero post ducenta, pietatis causa, devote visitasse. In quorum fidem praesentes litteras, sigillo eiusdem Sanctae Ecclesiae munitas, ei confert.

Compostellae die 25 mensis Junii   Anno Sancto Dni 2023

José Fernández Lago
Decanus S.A.M.E. Cathedralis Compostellanae

About the book

This book is about magic. The magic of an ancient pilgrimage in Spain, called Camino de Santiago.

In spring of 2019 I walked 500 miles from Saint Jean Pied de Port in southern France to Santiago de Compostela in Spain and then all the way to Finistere. It was while those 30 days that a process of my personal transformation was ignited. This flame burns still. It is an alchemical flame that can never be extinguished.

There, on that ancient road in northern Spain, I have experienced encounters for which I am still not sure what they were. Angels, ghosts, spirits, demons,…?

Most probably all of them. This ancient path has been made sacred by the millions of pilgrims who are in faith walking it for more than a thousand years. Here on the Camino, you have positive people walking it every day, 365 days, 52 week per year for more than a 10 centuries. Here you have a constant flow of energy for more than a thousand years. Because of this, the barrier between heaven and earth practically vanishes. This membrane becomes permeable and both worlds start to interfere. Sooner or later everybody on the Camino become aware of this – even the agnostics. Camino de Santiago is a living proof that in this secular world the sacred places still exist.

This book is a journal of my Camino. It tells the story about the people I met, it tells a story about my thoughts and my realisations and especially it tells about the spiritual events that have profoundly transformed my comprehension of the world.

I met people from all parts of the world. People from Germany, Switzerland, Sweden, Brazil, Argentina, Italy, Hungary, France, United States, South Korea, United Kingdom, Netherlands and Croatia. The largest group were naturally the locals from Spain. And I even meet two Slovenians.

I liked how equal people on the Camino are. It is not important who you are or what you do. Pilgrims only ask you for the name, so that they know how to call you, and where you are from, so that they know in which language they can talk to you. Nothing else matters. On Camino you are just a simple pilgrim. And this is so liberating.

Camino is about encounters. Some being short, some becoming a lifelong friendships. It is about a girl who's tattoos were telling the story of her hard life, it is about a young woman that has prayed being afraid of losing her boyfriend, it about an old lady asking me to embrace the saint in Santiago de Compostela also for her, it is about a man who lost and later luckily found his passport, it is about a love troubled middle aged woman that has burned in Finistere not just her clothes but also all the personal bridges, it is about a couple that walked to Santiago de Compostela from Hamburg, Germany and got engaged in front of the cathedral, and last but not least it is about the burden that I have caried and managed to let it go. It is about little villages and big towns, it is about roman bridges, it is about hostels and caffes, it is about trees, mountains and sky. Camino is love, faith and magic.

Camino is far from being just a walk. It is a unique multidimensional experience of a pilgrim traveling through three different phases: the physical, the mental and the spiritual one. The first two being a hard test of one's endurance and determination and the last one being a reword that pays out the first two for more than 1000 times.

Camino is really a unique experience. And for me Camino was definitely much, much more that I have ever expected.

About the author

Jorg K. Petrovic was born in Ljubljana, Slovenija in 1969. As economist by training he is author of many professional articles from his field of work in accounting, auditing and budgeting. This book is his first belletristic attempt. Through all his life he was interested in exploring metaphysical phenomenon such as ancient mysteries, henosis, mysticism and magic. In 2019 the ancient pilgrimage in Spain ignited the process of his personal transformation. He is married and a father of three daughters. Since 2022 he lives and works in Luxembourg.

www.ingramcontent.com/pod-product-compliance
Lightning Source LLC
Chambersburg PA
CBHW061337160726
47995CB00001B/61